T0368360

The **Supernatural**
World and Me

Spiritual Awakening and Psychic Development.
The reader learns to trust their intuition
and guidance from their Higher Self.

Martha G Klimek

BALBOA.PRESS
A DIVISION OF HAY HOUSE

Balboa Press books may be ordered through booksellers or by contacting:

Balboa Press
A Division of Hay House
1663 Liberty Drive
Bloomington, IN 47403
www.balboapress.com
844-682-1282

Because of the dynamic nature of the Internet, any web addresses or links contained in this book may have changed since publication and may no longer be valid. The views expressed in this work are solely those of the author and do not necessarily reflect the views of the publisher, and the publisher hereby disclaims any responsibility for them.

The author of this book does not dispense medical advice or prescribe the use of any technique as a form of treatment for physical, emotional, or medical problems without the advice of a physician, either directly or indirectly. The intent of the author is only to offer information of a general nature to help you in your quest for emotional and spiritual well-being. In the event you use any of the information in this book for yourself, which is your constitutional right, the author and the publisher assume no responsibility for your actions.

Interior Graphics/Art Credit: Martha G Klimek

Print information available on the last page.

ISBN: 979-8-7652-3946-9 (sc)
ISBN: 979-8-7652-3948-3 (hc)
ISBN: 979-8-7652-3947-6 (e)

Library of Congress Control Number: 2023903469

Balboa Press rev. date: 03/29/2023

Contents

Dedication

I dedicate this book to my husband Steve
for his encouragement to write this book.
Thank you, Steve
Wow, the second book in two years.
I would like to thank all the people who bought my first book.
Thank you, for all your kind comments and encouragement.
"Embracing the Supernatural and Paranormal Phenomenon
With Developing Your Psychic Abilities"
"How Does One Out Run the Supernatural
and Paranormal Phenomena?
You Don't. You Embrace It"

Thank you too all.
With Love,
Martha G Klimek

Website: marthaklimek.com
YouTube: Martha Klimek, or Embracing the Supernatural

Introduction

Over the years I have learned to embrace the supernatural world and not to fear it any longer. It took a lot of will power to accept the unknown.

As a child I grew up afraid of the two worlds I could see and hear. Adults including my parents told me that what I saw and heard was my imagination. No one believed me that Ghost did exist. As you could imagine this went on for several years.

My earliest recollection that I can remember to this day, is when I saw an elderly woman in my playroom. The lady told me to get out of the room. I was not very old at the time. I was scared of her. I went out to the kitchen and told my mother that there was a mean lady in the playroom. My mother said there was no one there, and to go back into the room and play.

The woman was getting more frustrated with strangers living in her house. I would hear and see her husband's spirit walking up and down the lane way. Sometimes I would hear him out on the veranda and I would think my father was home. Mom would say it was to early for dad to be home.

People kept telling me that no one was there and to quit lying, or it was my imagination. I soon learned to keep my mouth shut. I grew up in fear of not knowing I was seeing Spirits and Ghosts.

The teenage years were more horrifying. The sights and premonitions intensified to the extreme I thought I was going crazy. There was no one to talk to about this phenomenon.

One day I mentioned something to my father and he told me to forget all about it, and not to tell anyone about what I could see and hear. His one remark threw me for a loop. "They killed people for that." I followed my father's advice and did not speak of it. There was no way I could forget, so I tried to ignore it. Fat chance, that did not work. I went along with the premonitions and seeing the Spirits and Ghosts and I kept my mouth shut.

Recently I heard a Canadian Psychic on YouTube saying that until 2019 it was illegal to practice your Psychic Abilities in Canada. If you had a Psychic Practice, you had to tell the client their readings were for entertainment only. Under the Canadian Law it was classified as Practicing Witchcraft and the pretense to commit fraud. There were a few people charged under this outdated law. Mind you some of these people deserved it. They were committing fraud in the excess of charging clients thousands of dollars for various things.

In hind sight my father was protecting me.

As time went on, I would read cards for myself. I recently wrote my first book and had it published.

The book's name, "Embracing the Supernatural and Paranormal Phenomenon with Developing Your Psychic Abilities". "How does one out run the Supernatural and Paranormal Phenomena? You Don't. You Embrace It."

Most important the book shows the reader through many of the stories that there is a Spiritual Life After Death. Everyone has

Psychic Abilities. The book teaches readers how to develop their Abilities and what they see and hear is very real. The book shows the reader they are no different than the Professional Psychics. You can talk to your departed loved ones yourself and you already do it.

This book, "The Supernatural World and Me." Is about the Spiritual Awakening and Psychic Development it explains many topics of the Supernatural and Paranormal Phenomenon.

Chapter One

The book takes you through my journey of navigating the unseen world. Teaching the reader Psychic Development and Protection. Acquainting the reader with subjects like Old Souls, Empaths, HSPs, Meditation, Raising Your Vibrations, NDEs, Spiritual Awakening, and recognizing the signs from departed loved ones.

Chapter Two is teaching the reader about the Angelic and Spiritual Realm, Contacting Your Spirit Guides, and Angel Numbers.

Chapter Three is about Recognizing Energy, Energy Shifts and the Awakening State, and Energy Exercises.

Chapter Four is about Auras, Exercises to See Auras. Aura Cleansing.

Chapter Five is about Black and Negative Energy, Different Kinds of Ghost, Protection and Cleansing. Everyone comes in contact with these types of energies in their everyday life.

Chapter Six teaches the reader about Divination, Tarot and Card Layouts

Chapter Seven is about Astrology, Astrological Tarot Card Layouts, and Numerology.

Chapter Eight is about True Stories of Interactions with Spirits and Ghosts.

Meaning of Supernatural

What is the meaning of the supernatural? According to the dictionary and many people who have researched the subject of the Supernatural World, it means:

The manifestation of an event belongs to some force beyond the scientific understanding of Natural Law.

Supernatural is beyond the visible observation of the universe especially relating to God, a God, or Demigod, and artifacts people worship too, relating to the Spirit or the Devil, and anything too unusual to the laws of nature.

Some examples are miracles, magic and precognition.

Many other synonyms for the word Supernatural are:

Paranormal	Uncanny
Miraculous	Mystic
Psychic	Unearthly
Magical	Mysterious
Occult	Superhuman

The Meaning of Paranormal Phenomenon and Phenomena

The meaning of Paranormal or Phenomena refers to outside the scope of known laws of nature.

Many people have different forms of Psychic Abilities. The abilities can take the form of one of these known phenomena, Telekinesis, Clairvoyance, Psychokinesis, ESP Extrasensory Perception, and Telepathy. There are so many other abilities not mentioned here.

These events are beyond the normal scope of scientific reasoning. Trying to understand this phenomenon that is not of this world.

Many people can see and hear things, not of this world. These people are often called liars. They are ridiculed for their abilities if they come forward and use them. People with these abilities try to help others understand these things that are true and natural.

Often, children become aware of their abilities at an early age. Out of fear and disbelief, adults discouraged children from using these gifts. Parents have programmed ones with these gifts not to believe in Paranormal Phenomena. Children grew up believing that it was their imagination.

Chapter One

Shining the Light

How Does One Shine the Light?

One morning, I was in the shower meditating when I asked myself this question.

"Now that I have written this book and had the book published, what is next?" "How am I going to market this book?"

You know how your mind keeps wandering from one thought to the next quickly, making it difficult to quieten the thoughts in your mind?

Suddenly, I heard a voice say, "Shine the Light." I opened my eyes and looked around the room, knowing I was the only one in the room, but I still heard this voice, "Shine the light." A little shaken up, I finished up, went into the kitchen, and told my husband what had happened.

My husband still had a look of surprise on his face when I said, "How do I shine the light?"

He was quick to respond. Many of his suggestions were the same ones I just ran through my mind moments ago.

To list a few possible ways, let me see, to sell the book, you need to market the book, and how do I do that?

School taught you that Authors must market their books.

I need to find a way to get the word about the book out to the public.

I must find a way to speak about the book.

I need to create videos and post them on YouTube, Facebook, Instagram, and Twitter.

Speak to friends and family about the book.

I should approach bookstores and do book signings.

There are so many social media platforms, and the list keeps going on and on.

How will I be able to keep up with everything?

"Yikes." The one thing I did not consider, I am an introvert. How can a quiet and shy person do all these things? Slowly, by coming out of my shell.

"Help!" I get nervous speaking at public functions and try to avoid crowds. I do not know if I can do this.

It does not matter how you publish a book. You can publish it traditionally or self-publish it. You still need to have a marketing platform. A Publishing House expects you to market your book yourself.

It is necessary for the Author to have an email list and a large social media following, and do not forget about the speaking engagements. I have neither.

A writing course led to all this uncertainty. I did have a manuscript written in less than one year and ready to publish.

When the Publishing House telephoned and asked if I was interested in publishing my book, I had to say yes. After spending all this time and hard work writing this book. I could not say no?

The title of the first book I wrote is Embracing the Supernatural and Paranormal Phenomenon, with Developing Your Psychic Abilities. I wrote this book on Spirituality.

How does one outrun the Supernatural and Paranormal Phenomena? You Don't. You Embrace It!

The book is to bring enlightenment to people by telling them that there is a spiritual life after death.

When you are ready to leave this world, there is something to look forward to and not to be afraid of. The spiritual life is sharing our world as we live in it.

Many people see the spiritual world, and these people are spreading the word through many mediums, such as TV Shows, YouTube, and writing books.

YouTube is making it easier every day for people to come forward and share their experiences with their NDEs and shine the light.

They are spreading the word that there is more to this universe than we can see. How one shines the light is a good question. Everyone needs to come forward and start talking about their experiences.

I am going to try to shine the light, as requested. No! I need to shine the light.

My Road Through the Supernatural and Paranormal Phenomenon

How does anyone start on this road to the Supernatural and Paranormal Phenomena?

It's difficult to say it just happens. Scientists believe psychic abilities are in your genes, and people are born with them. Known Psychics have relatives that came before them who were no strangers to the paranormal. Mothers, Fathers and Grandparents pass the genes on to the next generation.

Many sensitive children to the Paranormal have grown up not knowing what it is. These children go to bed frightened and cowering under their blankets.

Some of these children were lucky enough to have someone to help them navigate the turmoil of the unknown, while others will not be so lucky. The unfortunate children have to wade through the unknown by themselves, because no one will take them seriously if they tell someone what they see and hear.

Some of these children will or have grown up being experts in Psychic Phenomena with lucrative careers. Some will prefer a quiet life and no recognition.

I was one child who grew up in fear after being told Ghosts did not exist. My parents and others did not believe me when I told them. Later, when I was a teenager, the sightings and hearing of Ghosts persisted. It even became worse. I did not understand what was happening. I became fearful of the unexplainable events that were happening around me.

At twelve, my instincts started to unfold with greater intensity. My grandfather passed away, and I thought it was my fault.

The year before, when I was saying goodbye to my grandfather, we were both crying because we knew we would never see each other alive again.

My family and I moved to another city a fair distance away, and unfortunately, we could not return for a visit before my grandfather passed.

We returned home after the Funeral, and the Paranormal became even more intense.

After I left home, I started to investigate the Supernatural. I started reading everything I could get my hands on. One day, I went to the library and checked out books on Supernatural Phenomena.

One night, after the children were in bed, I retrieved the books and started reading, that is when unusual things were starting to happen, so I closed the books and went to bed. After I fell asleep, the nightmares were frightening. I felt this incredible pressure on my chest, and I could not move or breathe. I became frightened, and I knew something was wrong. I started to pray and pray. The suffocation did not ease, and I continued to pray. The next thing I remember, I started praying in another language.

The pressure on my chest lifted, and I slept uncomfortably for the rest of the night.

I telephoned my aunt in the morning and told her what had happened the night before. I knew she would understand. I had overheard my parents talking about my aunt and me. My parents realized they could not deny I could see and hear Ghosts as my aunt could.

My aunt told me to close the books and return them to the library. She told me to pray to God and ask for his help to remove the evil I let in while I was doing my research.

I did as my aunt suggested. I decided then to give up reading tea leaves and tarot cards. Even though I was not participating in the Psychic practice, it never left me. I was still having visions, and my instincts were right. I kept this to myself and tried to live without my Psychic Abilities.

As I said, the abilities never went away. I tried to ignore my gifts, but that did not help. I have decided to embrace the Supernatural and Paranormal Phenomena instead of fearing them.

Being Psychic

What does it mean to be a Psychic?

Everyone would have a different point of view on what being Psychic means to them. Most would say their Psychic adventures started with the fear of not knowing what was happening around them. Some people were lucky, and they had someone to guide them. They were still frightened, and they tried to hide from this phenomenon.

When most Psychics tried to forget, or hide from the Spirits trying to make contact, they were unsuccessful. The Spirits never give up because Spirits know they can be seen and heard.

The Psychic Adventure starts escalating as children reach their teenage years. Some Doctors attribute this surge of Psychic Abilities to puberty, when the hormones change from being a child into becoming a man or woman.

At this point in some children's lives, they are starting to deal with the death of loved ones. Sometimes, these children thought they had caused someone's death when they foresaw it in advance. Some young Psychics tried to prevent the death. They tried to communicate unsuccessfully with the person in question. The person did not take the communicator seriously. In days, weeks or months, the death of their loved one happens. The young Psychic becomes frustrated and afraid. Self-doubt settles in. That is when Psychics are left wondering. Why do I have Psychic Abilities if I cannot change the outcome of a future event?

By the time the person with the abilities enters their twenties, they will become aware that they cannot deny they are Psychic. The person chooses to lead a quiet life and prefers to stay out of the limelight. Many Psychics will have a career in which they will not become famous, and others will become well known, maybe Psychics to the Stars.

The Psychics who make it to fame deal with ridicule and skepticism. The common phrase you hear them use. "You need to have a thick skin, and I do not listen to the Media. There's always the non-believers."

I chose the quiet life of not letting too many people know that I have Psychic Abilities. Time has passed over the years, and most people who knew have long forgotten, but that is okay with me.

For the longest time, I feared hearing and seeing the Spirit World. I have accepted what will be, will be.

Developing Your Psychic Abilities with the Five Clairs

How do you develop your Psychic Abilities?

Now that is a difficult question to answer. There are many different ways a person can be a Psychic. There is no good answer. It is different for everyone. Some people may have been born with their abilities, whereas others will have to develop theirs. The process can take a lot of time and be an arduous task. Everyone is born with psychic abilities, whether they know it or not. You have to find which one of the Clairs you are good at and develop that one. Maybe you have more than one Clair.

Clairsentience Clear Sensing

Clairsentience is the ability to be able to sense something. It is a way of feeling information and having gut feelings. You are sympathetic and empathetic. You can sense and feel others' pain. You feel tingling to notify you something is about to happen.

Maybe you have good instincts, and you do not realize it. I had a feeling, or your little voice told you. For example, you have had a good or bad feeling about something or someone you have just met. Your little voice tells you to buy the car or the house.

Sometimes you do not listen to your little voice or your instincts. You are afraid you may make the wrong decision while still weighing all your options. You think it is better to proceed with caution, and you will not take the chance.

In this case, it is time to keep track of all the times you were right or wrong. Keeping track can be a real eye-opener. A record will give you some insight into which ability you have.

I have been looking at cars to buy, and I sense this is the car I want to purchase. My husband has learned through the years not to question my feelings. I have a good track record of buying cars. My husband liked to pick out the vehicles until he picked a couple of lemons.

The only way to develop Clairsentience is to trust your feelings. Play the sensing game with cards. Regular playing cards will do. Try to guess what the cards are.

Buy yourself a Tarot Deck and handle the cards frequently. The more you play with your cards, the more the cards will pick up your vibrations, and get in tune with you. Try different card layouts. Read the cards using your intuition first. Check the book or booklet that came with the cards for correctness to see if you were correct. Being right is not everything. After a while, you will become quite familiar with your cards. Then use your intuition only.

Trust your feelings about what the cards mean to you. The more you do this, the better you will get at trusting your feelings. Practice is the key here. Keep a journal to record your accuracy and progress.

Clairvoyance, Clear Seeing

Have you been sitting quietly, and you saw pictures come into your head, or a flash of a scene playing out in front of you? You do not know why you had the vision.

As your ability develops, you will get these flashes anywhere and anytime, especially in the most inconvenient times. A picture flashes in your mind while driving, out with friends, or in school.

It can happen anywhere, and you cannot take the time to process what has happened. Have you been out to dinner with friends or family when you feel a little funny or spaced out? When you return to normal, you realize you missed a good part of a conversation. I have, and people thought I was not paying attention to them when they were talking to me. When I returned to the table talk, they thought something was wrong with me. How do I explain what happened? Will they believe me if I say nothing is wrong? Do I tell them I see things that are not there? I have learned not to press my luck with that one, mainly because I hide my abilities and do not want them to know I have them. Sometimes, I have had impressions of people having accidents. In these visions, the people sometimes do not live. Or the person has a terminal disease. Do you want to explain that to them? Not me!

Here are some exercises to try. They will teach you how to trust your instincts and help to get acquainted with your cards.

Pull out your Tarot Deck, go through the deck one card at a time and look at the cards. Concentrate on each card. What do you see? Look closer. Is there a scene playing out before you? Use your imagination. The more you do this, the stronger your intuition will get.

Trust your intuition. Practice, Practice makes perfect. Soon you will be able to do Tarot Readings without help. Keep a journal to record your accuracy and progress.

Here is an experiment you can try, visualize items, cartoon characters, or anything you want. Has it materialized in your mind? Another way to practice is to daydream. Who does not like to daydream?

Clairaudience, Clear Hearing

Have you ever heard someone calling you, and no one is around? Have you heard music when you cannot find the source? What about someone talking to you in your head? I mean, you miss someone who has departed. You hear their voice, or you think you are carrying on a conversation with them. You are talking to them. The loved one is so happy that they finally reached you.

In the rush of our busy lives, our loved ones have great difficulty getting our attention. Our loved ones come around quite often to be with us. We are too busy to hear them. Have you been driving somewhere and suddenly you hear, do not take that road or turn here, or maybe you hear stop so loud that it startles you, so you slam on the brakes? That is your loved one sitting in the co-pilot seat, enjoying your company and protecting you.

The key to Clairaudience is quieting your mind. Sit quietly, anywhere, with no distractions or with no background noise. Listen, what do you hear? Concentrate. Keep a journal.

Try this exercise often

Get into meditation. You must raise your awareness and listen to what you hear in your mind. Who comes to talk to you? Is it one of your departed loved ones? Acknowledge their presence. Maybe it is your Spirit Guide. Ask questions and trust what your mind hears, and reply.

Practice is the key here. Practice with meditation. A journal will help with recording accuracy and progress.

Clairalience, Clear Smelling

Have you ever smelled an odour that you did not like? Or did it make you want to be sick to your stomach? When you smell something that you know should not be there. Then you searched for the cause of the odour and could not find it. The smell is called smelly energy. It is a disgusting odour. You cannot wait to find out what and where it is. You know this odour should not be present in your home, and the unpleasant smell comes and goes. It does not linger for too long. That is when you know it is a ghost or a dark soul in your presence.

You want to pull out all the tricks of protection as soon as possible, to get rid of the dark entity. You can use sea salt, put the sea salt and water in a spray bottle, and lightly mist the rooms as you pray in each room.

Ask for help from your Spirit Guides, Angels, and your Higher Being. Mine will be God. You must tell this entity to go and never come back. Tell it, it is not welcome here. Be forceful.

Now there is another form of smelly energy. It can come from people with which you have come into contact. Their aura is not compatible with yours. Sometimes you cannot wait to get away from them. Maybe the person has a dark soul, an evil entity, and you can sense there's something off. The little hairs on your body stand up, and you cannot wait to get away from them. That person knows you know something is not right with them.

Now when the smell is pleasant and pleasing, you have no worries. The Spirit is a Spirit and not a Ghost. The Spirit may be one of your departed loved ones. Pleasant memories come rushing back to you of the person who wore that fragrance of aftershave. Was it your grandfather, father or husband?

Other triggers of memories are the smells of perfume, or the smell of lilacs, lilacs is the essence of a loving person. Cooking and baking aromas in the kitchen bring back wonderful memories. You remember the pleasant time you spent with your mother, grandmothers, sisters or aunts. You can smell these fragrances at anytime and anywhere.

You can experiment with this exercise

Use a blindfold. Cover your eyes to see if you can distinguish aromas from odours.

Clairambience, Clear Tasting

Some people can taste food or substance. Some of these senses or feelings can be pleasant or distressful. I have seen this done before on TV shows.

Sometimes, I can taste food when I have not eaten it. I thought it was a food craving. Other times I get the taste of something that is not food. Sometimes, there is something in the air, and I can taste it. Most of the time, it is not pleasant.

You can experiment with this exercise.

Use a blindfold as a test and see if you can distinguish the taste and what memories come to mind. Some people who are good at distinguishing taste, and they can taste individual ingredients in food. Now that would be something.

Taking Chances

Take chances when trying to develop your Psychic Gifts and your intuition. Keep a journal and write all your impressions down. No one has to know that you are doing it. Who cares if you are right or wrong?

Buy yourself a deck of Oracle Cards or a Tarot Deck.

Play with your cards.

Shuffle them frequently.

Handle your cards and study the pictures by looking at the cards. Read the definitions in the booklet.

Do you feel their vibrations?

When studying your cards, do you get impressions from them?

Write down your impressions in your journal. You can refer back to your notes at a later date. Compare your notes with your instincts. Repetition makes progress.

The more you practice, the better you will get at reading the cards and trusting your intuition.

Use these tools for yourself.

Remember when we were children, we used to play a game with a regular deck of playing cards. We used to try to predict the colour. Red or black, and we went as far as to try to guess the number.

The original Tarot Deck of cards was the regular playing deck, that we use to play cards today.

With the addition of the Greek deities, our card deck of fifty-two grew to a seventy-eight- card deck of Tarot Cards.

When you get better at reading what the cards mean, you can try it on someone you know and trust. Tell the person it is a game you want to play and not to take it seriously.

Believe it or not, when the cards made it into Europe, Tarot was only played for a pass time, like regular games. Only the wealthy could afford these cards. The cards were hand-painted illustrations and made out of paper.

The people with intuitive gifts realized that this game predicted future outcomes. Emperors of the lands used Tarot Cards to plan strategic and successful battles for their empires.

Take chances. Who cares if you are right or wrong? It is not likely you are going to become a famous Psychic. Who knows, maybe you will? Psychics start on their road through the Supernatural and Paranormal Phenomena by speaking to Spirits and predicting the future.

You can have fun along the way while improving your intuition.

The Afterlife

What is the Afterlife?

Many people do not believe in the afterlife. Why?

They have a difficult time acknowledging the Spirit World. They do not have faith that there was a spiritual life before we were born. They do not believe there is a spiritual life after this life on earth.

Many Psychic Mediums make a living by talking to departed loved ones of grieving families. These Psychic mediums are proof that there is life after death. Many people who do not believe in life after death, they have gone to events with other family members, and heard Psychic Mediums connect with the spirits of their family, or the Spirits of other families. The information given by Spirits was indisputably correct and opened the eyes of the non-believers. There have been many research studies that have confirmed there is life after death.

How do people change their minds about the afterlife? Many of these people are atheists and did not believe in the Spiritual World until they had a Near Death Experience.

After having an NDE, their Spirit returned to earth with the knowledge that there is life after death. In the last few years, many people have come forward and started telling their stories of their NDE.

It is amazing how many people have changed their minds after having a Near Death Experience. The numbers are staggering.

Many of these people had accidents in which they died for a

short time. Some died in surgery and returned to their bodies after a brief time away.

People who had Near Death Experiences returned to their bodies after travelling through a tunnel. Some people travelled very quickly ascending into the Universe. Some spoke of being in a dark void or something like that. These people who had these experiences have one thing in common, they left their bodies for a brief time, which may have seemed like a very long time to them.

Departed loved ones were there to greet the person with the NDE. After a short reunion, they return to their body. It was not their time to leave this world, and they still had work to do. Many returned to earth to spread the word that there is life after death.

Some people were fortunate enough to see Jesus.

I saw Jesus twice when I had my NDEs. Jesus was warm and comforting. He held his arms out to me so we could embrace and talk. All I remember from both conversations, it was not my time to leave earth, I had work to do, and I had to shine the light. I did not understand what I had to do. I did not want to return to earth.

I remember when I was a child sick in the hospital. A Catholic Priest would come by and sit with me every afternoon, and we would pray. This one afternoon, the Priest gave me The Last Rites. The Priest would leave after I had fallen asleep, and he would return the next day.

One day when I had awakened, I remember seeing Angels all around my hospital room. The room was all a glow with a bright white light. The Angels were standing everywhere, and they were singing. I must have fallen back to sleep because when I woke later, the Angels were gone. I asked the Nurses, "Where are the Angels?"

They told me no Angels were visiting me. Either the Nurses, Doctors, and maybe the Priest did not believe me, or they said they did not see the Angels because they had not. After I had seen the Angels, I started to get better. I know I saw Angels that day. I found feathers in my room. I was only a child, and who would believe me?

Old Souls

An old soul comes to earth to help the newer souls evolve. The older souls have been here many times before, and with each incarnation, they bring their wisdom of knowledge to earth.

A person with an old soul often isolates themselves out of confusion. They believe that people may think they are strange, stuck up, and do not fit into society. People often define old souls as unusual, eccentric, and weird.

Some old souled children do not feel comfortable interacting with people of their age, because the games or activities the children are doing seem childish. Children with old souls prefer to hang around adults because their conversations are more stimulating.

The characteristics of an old soul are:

You Tend To Be A Loner

They look at things vastly differently, and with more mature eyes than the other people around them.

An old soul does not have an antisocial temperament. They feel out of place and have the urgency to return home.

An old soul prefers to be away from crowds and people in general. The noise and crowdedness make them nervous and uncomfortable.

They do not feel comfortable in their skin and isolate themselves out of fear.

They enjoy solitude. This need for aloneness can also mean those old souls are aware that they have completed their lessons for this lifetime.

An old soul enjoys spending time alone at home, walking in nature, at the beach, or anywhere an old soul can find solace.

When an old soul is physically alone, they feel or sense there is another presence with them. They are not alone because they have the awareness their Angels, Spirit Guides, Loved Ones, and Ancestors are spiritually there with them, and keeping them company.

An old soul is a person who seems to feel older and wiser than their life years on this planet. An old soul feels this way because they have lived many lives before this life.

Your Thirst for Knowledge

An old soul is like a sponge, and they absorb everything that has a meaning in the universe.

An old soul is spiritually aware and likes to research spiritual topics. Old souls look to the cosmos to find higher self-awareness and impart their knowledge to others as natural teachers. Their soul is aware there is more to the physical world than people realize.

Their intuition is always on high alert, and they are confident that their intuition is correct.

Old souls are more in tune with their psychic abilities. They can see and sense there is more to this world, and the spiritual realms.

An old soul needs to know the true meaning of their purpose and inner fulfillment that money and possessions cannot buy. They do not define success as their sense of true meaning and purpose in this life.

You are Highly Intuitive and Spiritually Aware

As an old soul, your soul's intuition is in tune with you on the highest level.

An old soul knows they can advise people on multiple levels and age groups.

The old soul has helpful information to be used to make a difference in the person's life. When you receive this information download, you know that the knowledge is from your inner wisdom.

Claircognizant, the psychic ability of the sense of knowing, is very common in old souls. Your knowledge of things comes naturally to you.

You often find yourself over thinking things and analyzing the problem in every possible way. The obvious answer is always correct, but you want to think it through anyway.

Often an old soul has intuitive gifts of empathy, high intelligence, and a keen insight into human existence.

Well Grounded

An old soul is usually well-grounded and takes some things to the extreme.

Some old souls want to ignore their psychic abilities.

They have problems inter-grading the physical and Spiritual parts of their lives to create balance.

An old soul has a deep understanding and an attachment to the solar system. They know they came to earth to fulfill a mission and gather information for the higher source.

An old soul loves anything vintage.

People draw to you

Often, an old soul will find people come to them asking for guidance and advice. People trust an old soul's judgment and intuition because they weigh all the facts of the problem.

An old soul knows how to achieve the best outcome for the greatest good.

Old souls can see the big picture, and they let you know which is the best path for you.

An old soul has excellent instincts and determines what the truth is. They can see and read between the lines. A person cannot easily fool an old soul. An old soul can see through someone's motives and see the story within the story.

Old souls are older and wiser than they are despite their physical appearance.

Not Materialistic

An old soul enjoys the simpler things in life.

They are more comfortable being alone than in a group setting because they feel they do not fit in.

People do not understand crowds, and noise will disrupt an old soul's equilibrium. They cannot live within all that chaos, and an old soul prefers to live in a peaceful and quiet environment.

They love nature and the connection of earth's peacefulness with the slower-moving energy and tranquillity that soothes their souls.

Career Paths

Old souls are often found in careers and jobs that are engaging, and challenging with stimulation to feed their minds.

They make great teachers, writers, and artists, working in nature and jobs of a scientific nature.

Old souls need to make a difference by sharing and teaching their wisdom to the world.

People draw to old souls for their insights and wisdom.

They often can take the lead in situations that require the roles of an Adviser or Counselor.

An old soul reincarnated into this world with a mission to help other souls and do research for their higher self, and the higher source.

An old soul will pursue their higher purpose with enthusiasm and confidence. They will not fail.

Not Fitting In

Have you felt out of place everywhere you went? How could I feel this way? I always felt uncomfortable. Why was I the only one who could see ghosts? I speak to Spirits.

I could never find a logical explanation for why I was different. It is not that I am antisocial. I like people. I want to talk to them, but some things were better left unsaid. To be ignored is one thing but not to be heard is quite another. I would keep these visions and thoughts to myself.

I thought it had something to do with how I interacted with my parents. My parents had a saying, "Children are to be seen and not heard." You would think that type of thinking would wear off after you have reached adulthood.

When I go out to socialize, I still sit in a corner and observe everything. I still feel like an outsider and out of place. I get these visions or thoughts about the people there.

I could not understand why people did not understand me. Was it that obvious I was different from them? I pick up everyone's vibrations. Soon after reaching social gatherings, I would come down with a migraine.

Could people tell I could see and hear their inner thoughts? I was always trying to communicate with them from an intellectual perspective. People were not ready to listen to what I could see and hear. I guess they thought I was odd.

My parents, teachers and other adults I came in contact with thought, I was wise beyond my years. Some adults said I was an old soul. At the time, I did not know what an old soul was.

I could not escape from the shadows of Spirits. I could not overcome this overwhelming feeling. When I was in school and high school, I did not fit in.

We were always moving around, so new schools were always there to contend with. We moved to a larger city when I was in grade eight. It was the worst time of my life, school-wise. Boy, I did not fit in. I was new to a small secluded populated part of the city. The school was small, and only the residents of this area attended the school. The girls at the school did not like me living on their turf for whatever their reasons were. The girls of this school were MAJOR BULLIES. I could not go to school or walk down the street of this community without being attacked.

My mother called the Police, and they said they could not do anything unless they killed me. I did not understand what the girls' problems were with me. I stayed to myself. I did not talk to them.

They called me a coward because I would not fight back. They still kept up with these relentless attacks, day after day. I never engaged them in any way. They started rumours that everyone believed. It was pretty bad when the girls were physically fighting with each other. I was the one blamed for attacking them. A few times, the rumours reached my parents that I was the cause of the fight. My parents took the side of the other girls. My parents told me not to open my big mouth and not to put my hands on the other girls. I did not have to do anything, yet I was guilty and defeated without cause.

I learned from this experience I had no one I could count on, not even my parents. The parents of some of the girls talked to my parents. The parents said that the girls accused me of physical abuse, and the girls were going home with bruises. I never hit anyone. Where did the girls get the bruises?

About ten years later, I was cashing out the items I wanted to purchase, and the cashier asked me if I knew who she was. I looked at her and said yes. I knew who she was. The woman apologized for the abuse she inflicted on me. I was surprised and said thank you, and I left the store.

About twenty years later, I went to a Christmas Dinner with my mother. The dinner was held at the retirement home where my mother lived. We were sitting in the dining room waiting for dinner, and my mother told me that a woman who works at the Retirement Home was from the old neighbourhood.

Frankly, I told my mother I could care less. While my mother was praising this woman, I was ready to get up and leave. Then, dinner arrived at our table, and mother introduced us. Not to be rude, I looked at the woman and said hello. As the woman went on serving the other tables, she would pass our table and say sorry. I said to this woman, why are you apologizing?

I noticed she was in tears and crying a lot. She was having a hard time holding it together. Every time she passed our table, the woman said sorry. I did not want to ask the woman again why she was sorry. She knew why she felt guilty, and I knew why also. I did not want to relive those moments of torment again. My mother continued to praise her, and I returned to the moments of betrayal. The betrayal I felt when I was thirteen.

I have had dreams, astral visits and spirits of women who came to apologize, and I did not know why or who they were. I did not want to talk to them. Could they have been the girls from so long ago?

Through my research, I was able to define what an old soul is.

I felt I was out of place and that I did not belong here. At home, I grew up fast. I took care of my younger siblings when my parents were not home. There was never a dull moment. The siblings always wanted something, and the house needed to be cleaned.

Mother, Father and five children make seven, and I was the oldest. My parents were either working or out somewhere. Somehow, I managed to take care of my four siblings. I would get my siblings up in the mornings and feed them breakfast. I saw to it they were dressed and ready for school. I tried to clean up the breakfast mess before we left for school.

My mother was an unhappy person. She took her frustration out on all of us. My father tried in vain to ease my mother's unhappiness. That was not possible.

Our Souls have been around for eons of years. We can not pinpoint a year or date of birth because the ether or afterlife has no concept of time as we know it. Here on earth, we have a biological body that we use until we return to the other side when we pass away.

Many people I have seen before their passing have said. "See you soon." At one time, I have taken this comment out of fear. Did this mean I was going to pass away soon? I hoped not. Were they implying that their Spirits were coming to visit me from the other side? Yes, that is what they meant. Sure enough, their Spirit came to me so I could pass on information to their families.

My aunts and my mother said to me before their passing. "See you soon." Their Spirits came to me and told me everything was okay and not to worry. They were with loved ones who passed before them. I was happy and relieved. I passed their messages on to family members.

Researchers and colleagues refer to seeing you soon means that earth has linear time and the afterlife does not. One lifetime on earth is only a blink of an eye. We, earthlings, think life is a slow process of one year after another, until we pass on to the afterlife.

Are You an Empath?

Are you an Empath?

Empaths are people, who can detect the thoughts and feelings of others, places, animals, objects and plants. An Empath's innate ability to exchange energy or vibrations with other people. Empaths "Defies conventional science and psychology." Empaths not only discern people's emotional state and physical feelings. They also absorb people's energy or vibrations, which leaves an emotional and physical impact on the Empath. An Empath looks at the world from a metaphysical perspective, and they see the world through an abstract lens. Scientists have been at a loss trying to explain the metaphysics concept.

"According to a meta-analysis published in "Brain." Substantial Nero-imaging evidence shows that when certain regions of the brain are activated when we observe pain and suffering. A joint action of these regions facilitates an integrated cognizance of sensory, cognitive, and affective functions involved in empathetic pain. The findings of this research suggest that empathy is comprised of emotional feelings and simulated by inputs to the anterior insular cortex." The quote is from Jenna Smiley.

Empaths are similar to Highly Sensitive People. The difference is an Empath takes on the feelings of people. An Empath's brain is like a sponge.

Their brain soaks up all negative and positive emotions of each person. For instance, if an Empath attends a funeral, they take on the feelings of each person in the grieving family, and even all the people in attendance.

Everyone has empathy toward others, and that is always a given. Everyone can sense the joy, happiness and sorrow of others.

It is different for a person who is a Highly Sensitive Person or an Empath. They are more highly in-tuned with others' feelings. They can mirror the feelings of everyone they come into contact.

HSP people will not be physically affected as an Empath.

An Empath can feel the emotions of how a person is feeling without the person telling them. An Empath sees right through any pretense, even when the person is saying they are alright. An empath can sense and feel what the person is going through, even if it is a domestic argument or health problem. An Empath would make a great detective with their sharp intuition and empathy.

An Empath's brain is wired with electromagnetic neurons differently than an average person's brain. An Empath's brain has highly responsive neurons that mimic the other person's feelings. The electromagnetic waves in the brain transmit signals that an Empath can easily pick up.

These signals enable Empaths to experience and feel the other person's inner emotions on a deeper level.

With all the emotional ups and downs an Empath goes through daily, they need to be extra cautious with their health and protect themselves. An Empath has to set healthy boundaries when they spend time around others to prevent them from becoming overly stimulated and overwhelmed.

There are advantages and disadvantages of being an Empath.

Some advantages for Empaths are:

Empaths make good listeners and can make friends easily.

They have big hearts and tend to be generous with their time when it comes to their friends.

They truly listen and feel what their friend has to convey.

Types of Empaths

Emotional and Compassionate Empaths are the most common type of Empaths there are. These Empaths feel emotions more deeply than any other empathetic person, including Highly Sensitive People. Even though Empaths and Highly Sensitive People have many traits and qualities which overlap, they are in tune with themselves and others. They try to help in any way they can. They feel compelled to help.

Medical or Physical Empaths are more intuitive of others' aches and pains. They often can aid in the healing of others. The practitioner can receive an intuitive hit, sense where the trouble spot is, and use healing crystals or healing energy generated by their body to ease pain and make a diagnosis.

You should make an appointment with your own General Physician or Specialist for advice. Your own Medical Professional may have these intuitive qualities and use them in their practice.

There are Animal Empaths. They are Empaths who sense animals' emotions and use their abilities to treat and communicate with animals. An Empath can influence an animal's behaviour.

Fauna Empaths are in tune with all of nature and plants. They can sense the vibrations and connect to the planet, plants and trees.

A Claircognizant Empath

A Claircognizant Empath will look past a person's body and

verbal cues to find the person's true nature and intentions. This type of Empath understands what is on another person's mind by knowing and sensing what the person is thinking. No, a Claircognizant Empath cannot read your mind.

It is a feeling of intuitive knowing. It is the same as knowing something you have no previous knowledge of, and you know the answer. How did I know that information?

Psychometric Empaths

Psychometric Empaths can detect energy emanating from clothing, jewelry, pictures and other inanimate objects. Psychometric Empaths have aided in police investigations to locate missing people. They also use this type of Psychic Ability in their practice for clients for various reasons.

Empaths and Depression

Empaths come under strain with dealing with outside stimulation. Empaths come under the influence of depression by being overstimulated, and overwhelmed by others' emotions and problems. Empaths go into sensory overloads in crowds, excessive talking, noises, and smells. Other people's pains and fears are often felt emotionally and physically by an Empath.

Many Empaths will come under attack by being accused of being too sensitive, being dramatic, and labelled there is something wrong with them mentally. Manipulators will take advantage of Empaths. They will push them beyond an Empath's comfort zone and use them for their advancement and personal emotional dumping ground.

Empaths will exhibit signs of depression when they retreat to a place of calmness and peace. Signs of depression are nervousness, anxiety, panic attacks, social anxiety, tiredness, headaches, stomach aches, exhaustion and fast heart rates.

Some Empaths seek comfort in various ways, including seclusion, alcohol, food, drugs and other harmful habits.

Protection for Empaths

Empaths need to recharge their emotions frequently to avoid being depressed, or feelings of stress, and overwhelmed by everything that comes into their life.

A day can be overstimulating for an Empath. An Empath needs to set boundaries which include controlling the number of social functions they attend, and the number of people they interact with daily. They will try to avoid crowds at all cost.

An Empath needs to find tranquillity and no stimulation to cope. They do this by avoiding the radio, television, and people. They need to find a place of comfort, a softly lit room with no noise. Usually, this room is their bedroom or a place they feel safe to be themselves. A quiet walk by themselves sooths them. They need to meditate to calm and ground themselves. Dr. Judith Orloff encourages an Empath to embrace their heightened gift of empathy by cultivating emotional, intimate relationships, and increasing understanding of others and the world. Dr. Judith Orloff is an Empath, Psychologist, Author and teacher of Empaths.

Ways to Tell if You are An Empath

1. People say I am too sensitive, emotional, a basket case, and dramatic.
2. Friends and family come to me for advice.
3. People seek me out to talk to me.

4. I am a good listener.
5. People trust my advice.
6. My feelings get hurt more than others.
7. I feel sad if my friends are sad or hurting.
8. I dislike being crowded, and I am anxious when in crowds, it drains me physically and emotionally.
9. Loud noises, certain noises that bother me, or excessive talking tries my patience.
10. Being surprised or startled by people sneaking up on me.
11. Do I overindulge in alcohol, overeat, or use other excuses to cope with my emotional stress?
12. I can tell how people feel before they tell me.
13. Highly emotional movies, shows, and songs can make me cry.
14. I prefer not to socialize with a lot of people. I handle interaction better when I interact with one person. Or with a few people in attendance.
15. Being physically touched unexpectedly bothers me.
16. I can sense the energy around me.
17. I distract easily.
18. I need my alone time to keep myself in balance emotionally.
19. I get anxious when I do not get alone time, and when I am in crowds.
20. I get anxious when I meet people.
21. I can feel when things are off. I can feel when something does not feel right.
22. I know when someone lies to me.
23. People misunderstand me often.
24. I love it when I am alone or caring for plants.
25. I am artistically gifted.
26. I frequently get physically drained, especially when dealing with people.

If you can answer yes to most of these questions, you are an Empath.

Are You a Highly Sensitive Person, an HSP?

Most people are sensitive to a point. Some people are compassionate and do not let the world or personal events bother them. These semi-compassionate people are not HSPs or Empath.

Highly Sensitive People are sensitive to their surroundings, and everything around them can unsettle them.

After watching the World News on Television, a Highly Sensitive Person can become overwhelmed by grief or feelings of joy. An HSP has feelings of unhappiness, and they start crying and feel agitated or jumpy. Their moods can change quickly because their empathy affects their sense of well-being and balance.

Everyone has feelings that affect how they interact with their surroundings.

The feelings of HSPs' are easily hurt by insensitive people making negative, and rude comments to or about them. Once a comment is said, you cannot take back those hurtful words. You cannot undo the hurt feelings you may have caused another person. Some people do not care how they make others feel, and they can be cruel or vindictive.

Highly Sensitive People feel uncomfortable in a crowded room.

HSPs dislike the television's sound too loud. They do not like loud or sudden noises. These sensitive people can come off as being complainers and controlling. Sensitive people get overwhelmed by trying to fit into others' social lives. When there are many people at social events, their personalities will conflict with, or unbalance an HSP.

Dr. Elaine Aron, Psychologist, believes a Highly Sensitive Person has a higher and deeper sensitivity because of their central nervous system. HSPs' central nervous system enhances the reactions to external and internal stimuli like loud noises, lights and pain. The brain of a Highly Sensitive Person processes the stimuli more intensely than any other person's brain.

A Highly Sensitive Person will try to avoid violence, loud noises, bright lights and highly intense situations. They will have strong emotional, mental and physical reactions to the environment around them.

Some people will not understand the inconsistencies of HSPs because their emotions will be all over the place, and they will misinterpret an HSPs' sensitivity to everything. People will label them too sensitive, weird, and abnormal and try to shame them for how they feel. Highly Sensitive People are creative and gifted. They can see the world in a more insightful way than most people.

There are many advantages and disadvantages to being a Highly Sensitive Person.

The disadvantages of HSPs are people will consider them emotional wimps. People will try to walk all over HSPs. They see you as a coward, and you will not stick up for yourself.

The advantage is you can see everything more clearly. You are compassionate for humanity and the world in which we live. You see the beauty in everything, and you are more spiritually aware.

Researchers showed that a small percentage of the population, about 15 - 20%, are believed to be Highly Sensitive People.

The level of sensitivity determined in a Highly Sensitive Person may reflect how their parents, and mentors treated them as they were growing up. A nurturing home with love and support will greatly enhance the level of stimuli of a Highly Sensitive Person. They find pleasure and happiness in all things. A good cup of coffee in the morning, the sweet music of birds singing, and the pleasant smell of flowers will bring smiles to their faces. The quiet tranquillity of their home will ease their frazzled feelings of unbalance. According to Dr. Elaine Aron, about seventy percent of Highly Sensitive People are introverts.

Signs You Are a Highly Sensitive Person

Are you shy and often misunderstood?

When you were a child, did people say you were a loner, shy, or withdrawn?

Did they think you were being dramatic or overly anxious?

A lot of children were introverts in their childhood. They would rather be by themselves than put up with other people's drama.

Did you stay in your room when company came to visit?

As children, we daydreamed and had fantasies, and had imaginary friends. Were they imaginary friends?

My imaginary friends were visiting Spirits or ghosts.

A child processes information differently than an adult. Children can see the world so clearly and vividly. When a child tells adults about their experiences, the stories have more details and are colourful with enthusiasm. When a child grows into adulthood, they often have wild, weird vivid dreams that seem realistic.

Highly Sensitive People have deep emotions that can throw them for a loop.

A Highly Sensitive Person leaves home feeling physically well but suddenly feels ill after they attend a function. The HSP has picked up the emotions and vibrations of the people in the room. They became sick shortly after they were socializing with others. They were so overwhelmed by everyone's energies that they became physically ill and had to leave. They can feel the vibrations of other peoples' energies which imbalances them.

An HSP can sense a person's personality by looking at them and observing their mannerisms, facial expressions, and body language. An HSP can feel the vibrations of a person's aura by their inner knowing. Sensing other people's emotions can be very stressful for a Highly Sensitive Person's mind and body.

When an HSP gets overwhelmed, they lose a sense of their feelings and balance. When this happens, a Highly Sensitive Person must find peace and tranquillity somewhere quiet, most likely in their home.

When someone speaks harshly to Highly Sensitive People, it comes across as critical and demeaning. They are deeply hurt and take the criticism to heart. The negativity will disrupt their peace and harmony and give them an unbalanced feeling. HSPs will manifest physical ailments and self-doubt.

A Highly Sensitive Person has a very low tolerance for conflict and violence. They try to avoid it as much as possible. They cannot tolerate cruelty. When watching television, they prefer non-violent shows.

When there is conflict in the home, a Highly Sensitive Person can become physically ill, and mentally unbalanced from all this stress. They try to avoid stress as much as possible. They prefer to live a quieter and slower-paced life.

A Highly Sensitive Person will become very anxious under extreme pressure. Time constraints of having too many tasks to complete in a short amount of time will unsettle an HSP. They will start exhibiting a nervous tendency that makes them jumpy. They do not like to be startled in any way because it will imbalance their sensitive nature.

A Highly Sensitive Person will often show signs of withdrawal, shyness and wanting to retreat to their haven. Some Highly Sensitive People can be introverts and extroverts. Either way, how they present themselves to the outside world, they still need their alone time to unwind and regain their composure.

A Highly Sensitive Person will retreat to a low-lit and quiet room to recover from the pressure of the day's events. They need to relax their body's senses from overload, calm their emotions and recharge their mind and body for the next day's events.

A Highly Sensitive Person has an intolerance to pain.

They are overwhelmed by other people's emotions, which leaves their emotional reserves depleted or low.

Frequent body aches, stomach aches and headaches are common ailments for a Highly Sensitive Person. The feeling of illness comes on within seconds, depending on with who they have interacted with.

A Highly Sensitive Person gets lost in thought frequently. They mull over each event several times, hoping they did not overreact to a situation.

They over think even the smallest problem or idea and go over the event to ensure they did not make a mistake.

They do not want others to think poorly of them or have a reason to criticize them.

A Highly Sensitive Person holds themselves up to unachievable standards because they are their own worse critic.

They worry about how others will perceive them.

Am I wearing appropriate clothing?

Am I speaking intelligently?

Am I being heard correctly, or am I being misunderstood?

The list can go on and on. A Highly Sensitive Person's self-consciousness will go into a state of self-doubt and they start second-guessing themselves.

A Highly Sensitive Person despises change. Changes can turn their whole world upside down they will constantly fret about the situation. They will come up with different scenarios to help ease them into a new transition, like moving to a new home or a new job.

They need time to become comfortable with any new situation. A Highly Sensitive Person must have a regime to practice self-care. This self-care practice must help bring peace and harmony to them whenever they get overstimulated, and overwhelmed.

Meditation

What is meditation?

People meditate for different reasons, and meditating seems to be in demand and on the rise as more people attend meditation groups.

Meditation can be a form of self-reflection for some people, or one who tries to balance their inner emotions for physical and emotional well-being. Meditating has many health qualities. Meditation will lower your blood pressure. Meditation calms your mind, body, and soul and relaxes the body's nervous system.

Meditation quietens your mind before starting many kinds of work. Many Psychics meditate before meeting with clients in their office and doing Television Interviews.

Artists in many mediums meditate before they start a new project. These artists can be painters, floral workers or any other artist with artistic endeavours.

Meditation is used in several ways, sitting on the floor or chair or lying in a quiet place. You can sit on a cushion with your legs crossed in any position you wish; it does not matter as long as you are comfortable. Some people may prefer to sit on a chair because of physical ailments or preference. You do not need special equipment or clothing for meditation. Your clothes should be loose and comfortable.

You can sit at your desk and meditate by closing out the world for a few minutes per day, or as many times a day as you need to take a breather. Many professional people call this taking five to regroup their thoughts.

To meditate, find a comfortable, quiet spot and close your eyes. You can focus on a pressing matter to which you need answers. You may want to focus on an item as a focal point as you meditate. The time you spend meditating can be as short as a few minutes. It may be for a longer time. It is up to you to set the time you need to relax your inner self.

Close your eyes and take deep breaths focusing on your breathing. Deep breathing is most beneficial for getting the most impact. Breathe in through the nose and exhale slowly through your mouth. Concentrate on your problem or say a small prayer asking God, the Holy Spirit or your Spirit Guides for help for whatever your needs are at the time.

If you have no pressing need, you can pray to give thanks and gratitude. Your prayer does not have to be long; you can say just about anything in the way you choose by making up your prayer. God, the Holy Spirit and Spirit Guides will listen to you and your prayers. They are not looking for any structural way of praying as in Christianity. A simple prayer with your own words will suffice.

Yoga is a way of meditating by exercising as you focus on your breathing and posture techniques. Yoga will help you stay fit and relaxed, which is good for your overall health.

For centuries many cultures used meditations for many things, especially for Spirituality and self-awareness.

Meditating can increase your Psychic Abilities by focusing and opening the Inner Eye. The Inner Eye is known as the Third Eye. The Third Eye houses the pathways to everyone's Psychic Abilities. With practice you can open yourself to the Psychic World and Self-Awareness.

Raise Your Vibration

How Does One Raise Their Vibration?

Anyone can raise their vibration. All they have to do is be aware of the world around them. Energy is all around us. Every person and everything consist of energy and has a vibrational frequency. Once a person knows that everything consists of energy, they will be able to act accordingly and recognize it.

One good way to raise your vibration is to notice your surroundings. Notice the people around you. What do you feel about their vibrations? Are their vibrations higher or lower than yours? Do you get good vibes or bad vibes from the people around you?

Positive vibrations are a source of white energy. Higher and positive vibrations will uplift your mood when you are with a person or happy people. These people will make you feel good about yourself and give you a positive outlook on life. Life will look brighter and will uplift your mood and your vibrations.

Bad vibrations are a source of negative energy or black energy. Negative energy can come from a person having a bad day or having bad things happen to them. People with negative energy have lower vibrational energy.

The negative energy will affect a person with higher vibrational energy by casting a shadow of darkness over the person. The dark shadow will impact a person's vibrational energy by lowering it.

People with dark energy do malicious things on purpose without remorse for hurting people.

A person who wants to raise their vibration has to protect themselves. People can use many techniques to protect themselves from other people's vibrational energy.

Protection

One way is by showering or bathing daily to wash all negativity from your aura. Your aura may have picked up the negative energy when you were socializing or from your co-workers. Why do you feel so much better after a bath or shower? Bathing or showering washes your aura. It is refreshing, and you feel much lighter and calmer.

Some people use this saying in their daily practice of cleansing themselves.

"I am washing all the negativity down the drain."

Visualize all the negativity running down the drain with the water and soap suds. Your body and aura feel brighter, lighter, and cleaner. In my opinion, it does help me.

Try hanging out with happy, upbeat, and energetic people to raise your vibration. I know it is not always possible to be with people who maintain a positive outlook on life. A change of friends may be in order.

Visualize yourself standing in the middle of a circle of mirrors. Have mirrors surrounding you. Have all the mirrors' shiny reflective sides facing away from you. The mirrors will reflect all the negativity away from you. You can do this protection method first thing in the morning before you leave home for the day. You can do it at any time of the day when you come into contact with negative people. It only takes seconds to put the protection into place.

Another way to protect yourself from negativity is to use the cloaking method. Visualize a bright white light of the Holy Spirit covering you or surrounding you. The negativity cannot penetrate your protective shield. You may have to do this several times a day when you feel your energy is a little low.

After you have protection, you can move on to more positive ways to raise your vibrations.

Stimulate your mind with positive affirmations. Be kind to yourself.

When a negative thought comes into your mind, replace it with positive and happier intentions.

Read uplifting literature, have positive conversations and hang out with happy people.

Be kind to others.

Think kind thoughts of others.

Share with others without any expectation in return.

Go for a nature walk.

Bring nature inside with flowers and plants.

Notice the beauty in everything and everyone.

Some people use candles, incense, and scented water to refresh their atmosphere and aura.

Be grateful and recognize your abundance.

Abundance is not what you have or your wealth.

Abundance can be a person who has good health, a place to live, and a job with enough money to pay your way, and for the things you need to live comfortably.

Write gratitude lists to remind you of the abundance you already have. Gratitude lists are positive ways for you to raise your vibration.

Meditate to bring peace and calm into your life. Do not stress, and stay calm, things will work out eventually. Meditation raises one's vibrations by one listening to their inner self and bringing peace within.

Breathwork for meditation and exercises are important for your emotional and physical balance.

Trust your emotions and set positive intentions.

If something does not feel right, then do not do it.

If someone does not have positive vibrations, leave that person or the area as soon as possible.

Remove yourself from drama.

Listen to upbeat music. It will uplift your emotions and make you feel good.

Dance if you can.

Daydream of pleasurable events or things.

Visualize you are on vacation, or of anything that makes you happy.

Smile, laugh, dance, and sing frequently. Have fun!

Ego

What is the Ego?

The Ego is the part of you or any person that it can pertain to:
This is a quote from Google.

""I" or the self of any person, a person as thinking, feeling, and willing, and distinguishing itself from the selves of others and objects of its thought."

"An inflated feeling of pride in your superiority to others."

The Difference Between Ego and Attitude:

When a person does not monitor their Ego, the behaviour of the Ego will become negative energy, and it can destroy you.

Attitude is positive energy that will sustain you.

The Ego in Metaphysics is conscious of the thinking subject.

Defining the Meaning of Ego:

1. Self-esteem is the way a person feels about themselves. It could be a positive or negative thing. A person can feel comfortable about themselves, or they can have a negative feeling which deflates their motivation, and positive feelings to accomplish a positive outlook on life.
2. Self-importance is how a person feels about how important they feel in general about themselves or when they measure themselves to another person. A negative emotion would be that the person will never surmount to the aspirations of others.

3. Self-worth is when someone elevates their monetary worth to another person's wealth.
4. Self-respect is how the person feels about themselves. The Ego can be positive or negative. It all depends on which way the Ego influences the person's consciousness. A positive emotion would be when a person respects, and looks after themselves by thinking positively, and taking care of their body. The negative emotions would be the opposite, demeaning thinking and abusing their body.
5. Self-conceit. The person's consciousness measures their self-importance. Some people think that the only person that has any importance is themselves. The person is always in the place of using I, I, I, and everything is all about them, and never giving regard to others' feelings.

The Ego is part of your subconscious that mediates between the unconscious and the responsible for reality testing the sense of personal identity. It operates on the reality principle of maintaining realistic and socially appropriate behaviour.

What is a Healthy Ego?

A healthy ego is when one is not judgmental of themselves and exaggerates their achievements and abilities. The person maintains a positive outlook on life. They can face any challenge with confidence. The person can admit they are wrong and say sorry when needed.

A negative ego comes from emotions that the person has to be correct and prove they are right even if they are wrong. They are always justifying themselves in how they think and act toward others. They need to judge.

When the Ego has a positive mental attitude, the person does not need to chase down or attack others when someone has done wrong to them. Road rage is an example of how the incident could take a positive or negative turn. When a person cuts you off in traffic, you ignore the incident, or you chase down that person and try to get even, verbally or physically.

The definition of Ego has a negative denotation of being arrogant, proud or selfish. The Ego is neither positive nor negative. It is up to a person's conscious and moral compass and how it will rationalize the appropriate social behaviour.

There is nothing wrong with having an ego, every person has one. One has to learn to control it. Your Ego can be helpful as your moral compass, keep you on the right track of acceptable social behaviour, and guide you when problems arise, and not going your way. The situation will affect your decision-making and mood, or they could turn you into a victim. A negative egotistic ego can make the person act as if they are superior to others to justify their behaviour.

Signs of An Inflated Ego:

1. They always have to be correct.
2. They are never satisfied. They always want more.
3. They do not like competition. They always need to be the winner.
4. They require constant recognition.
5. They have one-sided conversations.
6. Their opinions are the only correct opinions, and they do not validate others' opinions.
7. They lack empathy for others.
8. They are attention seekers. They have to be the focus of the party.
9. The person is full of himself and self-absorbed.
10. You overestimate your abilities and self-worth.

11. You underestimate the required skills and efforts to achieve your goals.
12. Loss of reality and missed opportunities to improve oneself.

Ways to Keep Ego in Check:

1. Take responsibility for one's actions.
2. Change your attitude when you can.
3. Stop beating yourself up when you make a mistake.
4. Focus on your growth, personally and professionally.
5. Take care of one's self, physically and emotionally.
6. Stop negative thinking and speaking about yourself.
7. Always show kindness to others.
8. Do not value other people's opinions above yours. (negative, or positive)
9. Practice Self-awareness. Acknowledge one's thoughts and feelings. Monitor behaviour.
10. Pause and think twice before taking action, engaging in arguments or saying something you will regret.
11. Relax and do not take things personally. Constructive criticism is motivating and will inspire you to do better.

The First State of Ego:

The parent of a child teaches the child how to act, think and feel. Parents, teachers, or mentors built this foundation of behaviour taught to children.

Your parents are the ones who set boundaries and implement the rules for you to follow. They showed you how your feelings worked. Where did your parents get these rules that they follow? The teaching of regulations and acceptable social behaviour came from their parents, and parents leading back centuries.

The Second State of Ego:

In the Adult State, the Adult is on a fact-finding mission and implementing the facts as they determine is right for them. They prefer to follow their instincts rather than use their parents and childhood traditions.

The Third State of Ego:

The ego state of a child contains all natural feelings, needs, impulses and potentialities as an infant. The Ego of the child learns how to be creative and manipulative. Children are aware of their intuitive capabilities, emotions and behaviours.

Children learn from their parents and mentors and their teachers to manifest traits like compliance and procrastination.

Anti-social behaviours like anger and inflated egotistic behaviours start to merge into their characters.

People with negative egos do not learn from their mistakes. They are self-denial and cannot own up to their mistakes, and have the need to blame others. The egotistic behaviour often descends into hatred and resentment.

Weakness of Ego:

The weakness of an Ego is the inability to control impulses and tolerate frustrations, disappointment and stress.

Signs from Your Loved Ones and Angels

Everyone receives signs from their loved ones. You may not be aware of the subtle signs. Sometimes the signs from heaven are small, and you do not notice them.

Scents

The most common sign is when you smell something out of place in your environment.

Pleasant smells of cologne, aftershave, perfume, someone's favourite flower scent, smoke and cooking aromas are the scents you remember of your loved ones.

These scents will take you back to more pleasant times, and memories when you were with your loved ones before they passed.

Finding Coins

Many people find coins in unusual places. Sometimes these coins will turn up unexpectedly in a place you knew they were not there.

People call this "Finding Pennies from Heaven." The coin can be any coin. It does not have to be a penny. When you find coinage in unusual places, take a closer look.

Notice the date and metal of the coins. Are there distinctive markings on the coin? Did someone special to you have a connection to certain coins?

Does the date on the coin have a special meaning? Does the date remind you of an anniversary or birthday? Is the date significant to both of you?

Remember the time and what you were thinking about when you found the coin. The coin has a special meaning of love and support from a loved one who has passed on.

Maybe the coinage is from your Spirit Guide or your Angels. The Spirit is reminding you they are with you and you are loved.

Hunches and Whispers

At times you will have funny little feelings and hunches.

Sometimes you may have someone whispering in your ear. The Spirit whispering in your ear could be a departed loved one, one of your Angels or Spirit Guides.

They are all here to guide you and protect you. They bring you wisdom and inspiration.

They may be there to guide you through some of your most difficult times.

The Angels may be with you to help heal your mind, body and soul.

Listen to your hunches. You may be able to tell who is there whispering in your ear. Pay close attention to hints, nudges, your feelings and repetitive messages.

A Spirit is trying to communicate with you.

White Feathers

When you find a white feather, and any coloured feather in an unusual place, a place where you would not find a feather, pay attention.

The Angels are there to help, protect and support you.

I say any colour feather because Angels have different coloured wings.

Finding feathers has the meaning of reassurance and encouragement. Your struggle is almost over.

Flashes of Light

Spirits of the afterlife, Angels and Spirit Guides can be flashes of light. These flashes of light can be shimmers of light, and sparkles you see out of the corner of your eye. A shaft of light surrounding you, or near you means Angels are visiting you.

Mirrors can glint light without a source of light reflecting into it.

Orbs can indicate the Spirits, Angels and Spirit Guides are with you.

Pictures and video recordings can have little white orbs without any source for lighting. The Orbs can be of loved ones when taking group pictures.

These signs of light come with the meaning of having faith in yourself. They also mean strength, wisdom, and creativity to succeed is within reach.

Spirits do affect electronics, and lights may flicker when Spirits are around.

Direct Messages

You can get direct messages from the Spirits of your loved ones, Angels and Spirit Guides in many different ways.

There may be a message on a billboard that means something to you.

The information can come from Magazines, newspapers, and books.

A book falls off a shelf by itself and lands on the floor. When you pick up that book, the book is open to a page, you read a paragraph or the first line of the page, and it has meaning for you.

You know it is a divine message meant for you.

Tingles, Goose Bumps, Chills, Hot Flashes

Tingles, sensations like goose bumps, chills, and warm sensations around your head, neck, shoulders, upper back and arms are signs from your Spirits, Angels, and Spirit Guides that they are nearby. They are around you and want to get your attention.

Sudden warmth and tingling when your feet fall asleep are indications that Angels are trying to raise your vibrations closer to their level.

When sudden temperature changes happen while you are meditating or praying are sure signs the Angels and Spirits are with you.

All these sensations are to raise your awareness, and you are on the right path.

Dream Visitations

Spirits of loved ones, Angels and Spirit Guides will visit you in dreams, and give you messages. Sometimes, the information is easy to figure out, and sometimes, you will not know what it means until some time in the future.

The Spirit World has no concept of time, they do not have time constraints like humans.

The Spirits visit when we sleep because it is the only time our mind is quiet enough to hear the Angels.

Throughout the day, the hustle and bustle of living life prevent us from hearing the Spirits and Angels. We cannot hear or see the Spirits with all the daily noise we have in our life.

Music and TV

Sometimes we will get messages through music and television from our loved ones, Angels and Spirit Guides.

The radio and television can suddenly turn themselves on. Switch channels on their own and act bazaar. Electronics can act so weird that we think they need to be repaired or replaced.

With radios, the music can be playing a song that reminds you of your loved one who has passed on. The song playing can have a message that only you will know what it means. Sometimes you will get only static on the television or radio. Your loved one or Spirit Guides, and Angels are trying to make contact, and they are having great difficulty. They are trying to get you to go quiet so you can receive their message.

You may stumble into a television or radio program of interest and think it was by accident. It was no accident. The Angels were getting your attention to receive their messages and keep you on the right path.

Nightly Encounters

Your loved ones, Angels and Spirit Guides are frequent fliers. They love to visit you at night.

Have you been waking up frequently at a specific time at night? The Spirit World is trying to get your attention.

Sometimes, the time on the clock can have a significant meaning for you and your loved ones. Maybe, it was the time of their passing. They are there to tell you they love you and have not forgotten you.

Maybe, the message they are trying to convey is a warning, or it is to help you with something. They are there to say hi, I love you and support you.

It is a nudge to keep you on the right track.

Random Coincidences

Coincidences are not random. They happen for a reason.

What about butterflies, dragonflies, birds, robins, blue jays or anything that has some meaning for you, or your loved one? They show up when you least expect them.

These things are happening around you more than usual, and they are unusually close, and there is no doubt they are there for you.

These are not coincidences. They are there to say hello, I love you, and you are not alone.

They are showing you the beauty and the love in your life. Slow down and pay attention, so to speak, and take the time to smell the roses. I love you. I am watching over you.

Another example is you can be looking for something. You cannot find it anywhere. You cannot purchase the item you need. Then you are out, maybe at a yard sale, and you find that item. Is that a random coincidence or a divine intervention?

Ringing in the Ears

Do you have ringing in your ears? Ringing in the ears usually is not a medical problem. Ringing in the ears usually means your Angels, Spirit Guides, and loved ones are trying to make contact. It is called a download. The ringing in the ears can be in the form of quiet whispering, bells ringing, and loud or buzzing sounds, and these are all called downloads.

The downloads contain information that will come to light without you knowing it until you need the information.

Telephone Calls

Your loved ones, Spirit Guides and Angels are trying to get your attention through telephone calls.

Sometimes, the telephone call will be full of static. You may get these telephone calls any time, day or night.

The telephone calls may come in at the time of a person's Birthday or on the anniversary of a loved one's death.

The Spirit World tries to get in touch with you in any way they can, to get you to listen to them.

Nowadays, it is difficult to tell where any telephone call originates. There are so many unlawful people trying to defraud the people of every country. You know the telephone calls, the ones, the missed calls with no caller ID. When you call that number back, thinking it might have been an important call, the voice at the other end of the line tells you they did not call. Or the number you are calling is not assigned. What is with this?

People are piggybacking off your number.

Back in the seventies, we had none of this. I remember a few times I picked up the phone when there was nothing wrong with it. It had to be a Spirit on the other end of the line.

Sometimes, the call was so full of static that you could hardly hear the voice on the other end. Sometimes, the person's voice is distant and weary but familiar, and the voice of a loved one's Spirit. Just as you recover from the initial shock, the voice fades away, and the message is lost.

Before, you used to be able to distinguish unassigned, and weird numbers from legitimate numbers but not now.

Your intuition would tell you that a telephone call was from the Spirit of a loved one. Not anymore.

Noticing the Beauty

Sometimes, your loved ones, Spirit Guides and Angels will nudge you to take time and notice the beauty around you. You pause long enough to look at nature, a beautiful sunset, and animals of all kinds. They remind you to stop long enough to smell the roses and take in all the beautiful wonders of the world.

Angel Numbers

Angel numbers are another way the Angels, Spirit Guides and your loved ones are sending you messages. These unique numbers appear in sequences of three or four repeating numbers. Sometimes, the numbers can appear in ascending and descending numbers.

These numbers are like 1,2,3,4, and then you can reverse the numbers as 4,3,2,1. Each set of numbers has its vibrational frequency and special meaning.

Angel numbers and what they mean will be in another chapter.

Butterfly Feelings

Butterfly feelings in your solar plexus are another way you can tell that your Angels, Spirit Guides, and loved ones are near you.

You know the feeling when you get that fluttering feeling in your stomach and slight chills? The Angels are just letting you know that they are with you.

Maybe your ears will start ringing. The Angels are getting you ready for your download. The Angels are telling you to pay attention to your surroundings.

Watch what you are doing, and they are there to let you know you are loved.

Babies and Animals

Babies and animals are very intuitive. They can sense when Angels, Spirit Guides and loved ones are present. You can see your baby's eyes light up, or the baby is looking over at a corner of the room. They are smiling and cooing at no one.

Babies are known to wake in the middle of the night. They are cooing or talking to no one.

There were plenty of times I walked in on my children when they were younger, and they were talking and playing with some unseen person. When I would pick them up, their eyes fixated on a corner of the room. I would look over there and say hello. All children and animals are like this.

My sister told me the day her youngest child was in a traffic accident. She could have sworn their son came in from work that morning, and he was playing with the dogs. It was not unusual for them to hear their son and dogs playing every morning.

When my sister's husband opened the door to Police Officers that morning, he thought they had the wrong house.

Many strange things have happened since that day. The dogs appear to be playing with an unseen person.

Their daughters can sense when their brother is standing there with them when they do their hair, and makeup before going to work each morning. Then the dogs start playing with no apparent person as they leave the house.

Feeling not Alone

You know the feeling you are not alone when you are alone. There is no physical person with you. You still feel you are not alone.

Well, you are not alone. You are never alone. Your Spirit Guides, Angels and loved ones are with you. You cannot see them, but you can sense them. You can catch a glimpse of them out of the corner of your eye, or you can suddenly look up and you see something, and it vanishes quickly. You stand there and wonder who was standing there. I do this countless times a day.

I wish I could physically see the glimpses of Spirits, and they were not just indistinguishable flashes. I would love to visually know who the Spirit is, when I talk to my loved ones.

You are never alone, and you should not be afraid. Spirit Guides and Angels are our protectors and they are here to keep you company and protect you.

Your Intuition is Your Antenna

Your intuition lets you know that you are not alone. Your intuition is your antenna, and it will never fail you.

Your Spirit Guides, Angels and loved ones are definitely on your radar. You can sense them all the time, even when you are sleeping.

You are never alone. Pay attention, and you will be able to communicate with them telepathically.

NDEs

More people are coming forward with their own experiences of NDEs, seeing Angels, and travelling to wonderful and glorious places that have no comparison to anything on earth. People said they were visiting with their dearly departed loved ones, and they had to return and complete their mission.

Many of these people have returned to earth without knowing about their mission. They believe their mission is to tell people that there is life after death, maybe not in the same way we know it now, but there is definitely a Spiritual life to look forward to.

For the longest time, people have believed that no person would have laid their eyes on Jesus. People are seeing and having conversations every day with Jesus, when they have their NDEs.

I have seen Jesus three times. Twice when I had Near Death Experiences, and once when I could not wrap my head around how people of any era could be so cruel and murder other people. I was a child in the hospital when I saw Angels, and the two other NDEs were as an Adult.

Both times Jesus told me it was not my time to leave this world, and I still had work to do. All I can remember from the conversations it was not my time to return to heaven, and I will remember our conversations when the timing is right. I remember Jesus's warm embrace, and we did have a conversation.

Maybe, I was to write some books, and shine the light on whoever is willing to listen and help them prepare for the new world.

I have seen the glorious sights of Heaven, Angels and departed loved ones on the other side of the veil. This place is a magnificent sight to see and has confirmed that there is life after death.

The accounts of a one person's NDE can be vastly different than another person's NDE.

All I know is the Angels, Jesus, and Heaven will always be there.

Spiritual Awakening

After World War Two, Spiritual people believed there was a Spiritual Awakening. The Higher Source and its Spiritual Beings are helping prepare people for the new world. The new world is for anyone willing to listen and prepare for it Spiritually. The Spiritual awakening has been evolving for many years.

In 2012, many people thought the world and earth would cease to exist. Instead of the world ending, people believed there was a new dawn of the Spiritual movement. Many on earth started to evolve Spiritually. People became comfortable talking about their spiritual experiences and shining their light. These people are letting others know there is more to look forward to when they leave this world. The new world is only a dimension away.

Spiritual Research Scientists believe Spirits live simultaneously with us. Spirits live on the other side and this side of the veil on earth.

I believe that the spirit world is living in this world. We see a world of upheaval and distraught for many. Many people do not want all the chaos in their everyday life.

Spiritual Research Scientists believe unhappy people have taken their lives because they cannot live in all this turmoil on earth.

It is the belief that their soul will have to return and live another lifetime here on earth to complete their evolution. There is more on this subject in later chapters.

Chapter Two

Archangels

Who Are and What Are the Archangels?

There are Seven Archangels.

The Archangels are in the existence of truth and faith.

Their presence in the Bible is incontrovertible testimony.

Angels and Archangels are incorporeal beings God created to be his servants and messengers. The Angels are attentive listeners and executors of God's Command. These spiritual beings exist for Him and in Him.

The three Archangels known as Michael, Gabriel and Raphael occupy the highest domains of the Angelic Hierarchy, and their duties are more significant than the other Angels.

Although Archangels still perform similar tasks as other Angels, the Archangels will interact with the physical world and the human aspects of life.

Archangels are the Heavenly Hosts and the driving force of all the Angels. The Archangels can implement changes, and they have the power to stop opposing forces. Archangels in the Bible are known as the Watchers of humanity and all affairs.

The Catholic Church recognizes three Archangels in the scriptures and these Archangels are Archangel Michael (Who Is Like God?), Gabriel (God's Power), and Raphael (God's Doctor).

Archangels usually work with larger groups of people, although that does not mean you cannot call upon an Archangel for help. Each Archangel and Angel have expertise in specific job categories they can use to help you.

The Catholic Church believes this is the correct number of Archangels that have been verified according to and stated in the Holy Canonical Scripture.

When you look at the Book of Enoch, several more Archangels are listed. The Archangels in the Book of Enoch are Uriel, Raphael, Raguel, Michael, Phanuel, Sariel, and Gabriel.

These are the seven Archangels in the text of the ancient tradition of Judaic origin.

In Mesopotamia's Babylonian Civilization, there were five Archangels instrumental in dealing with the fallen Angels, and these Archangels were Raphael, Uriel, Zerachiel (Saraqael, Baruchel, Selaphiel, and Sariel), and Ramiel (Jerahmel, Juhudial, or Jeremiel) and Raguel (Sealtiel).

Archangels can have many different names depending on the Religion, and the spelling of their name can also vary on the Religion practiced.

Archangel Michael (Who Is Like God?). Archangel Michael is also known as Mikal, Mika'il, Beshter, Sabbathiel and Lord Michael in multiple Religions and beliefs.

Archangel Michael is known as the armoured-wielding warrior. Archangel Michael fights against Satan and his emissaries. Archangel Michael is the defender of all who loves God. Archangel Michael is also the protector and patron Saint of Police Officers.

Archangel Michael protects all that is good and all that is good for the highest good of all. Archangel Michael is the Archangel to turn to when you need to find the truth and guidance. Archangel Michael is fearless, courageous, and our Spiritual Protector. Archangel Michael is the defender of the faith and the Church. When you see flashes of blue or purple light, Archangel Michael may be in your presence.

The Four Corners, the Four Directions, or the Four Winds are alternative names referring to the Cardinal Points.

Archangel Michael's Cardinal Point is South

Archangel Michael's Mystical Traits
Colour: Sapphire Blue
Crystal: Lapis Lazuli, Azurite, Dumorierite
Chakra: The Throat Chakra
Element: Fire
Zodiac: Virgo, Scorpio, Leo, and Capricorn
Planet: The Sun
Day of the Week: Sunday

Archangel Gabriel (The Power of God or God is Mighty). Archangel Gabriel is known as Jiburili, Gravriel, Jabrail, Gibrail,

Jibril, or Djibril. Archangel Gabriel is one of the closest spirits to God and sits on the left hand of God before his Heavenly Throne.

Archangel Gabriel is the Angel who revealed that the Virgin Mary was going to have the son of God, and he was to be named Jesus.

Archangel Gabriel revealed to Daniel the secrets of God's plan.

Archangel Gabriel announced to Zechariah the birth of John the Baptist. Archangel Gabriel is also known as the Angel of Death.

Muslims believe Archangel Gabriel is the Chief Messenger of God, who revealed the Koran to Muhammad.

In some beliefs, Archangel Gabriel is the Angel who will blow his horn to announce Judgment Day, according to the Apocalypse of John.

Archangel Gabriel is the Angel of communication and the protector of postal people, ambassadors, journalists, and couriers.

In pictures, Archangel Gabriel is a young winged cherub with a white lily in his hand. A white lily is the symbol of the Annunciation of Mary.

Archangel Gabriel works along with other spiritual guides for the care of children. Archangel Gabriel will aid in pregnancies, adoption and the general upbringing of children.

When you need clarity on something troubling you, all you have to do is call on Archangel Gabriel for assistance and advice.

Archangel Gabriel is the Divine Messenger of all other messengers, and these messengers will come in the forms of teachers, writers, artists, counsellors and actors. Archangel Gabriel will guide you by giving you, insight, inspiration, nudges, and motivation to complete your artistic work and messages.

Archangel Gabriel will provide you with guidance for your career choices.

Call on Archangel Gabriel to help you when you experience blockages. Writers and Artists often face blockages and need help with inspirational ideas.

If you feel you are in a rut and you think that you are making no progress moving forward, call upon Archangel Gabriel.

Archangel Gabriel's Cardinal Point is West.

Archangel Gabriel's Mystical Traits
Colours: White, Indigo, Orange.
Crystal: Clear or Snow Quartz, Agate, Selenite.
Chakra: Sacral Chakra, Crown Chakra.
Element: Water.
Zodiac: Scorpio, Pisces, and Aquarius.
Planet: The Moon.
Day of the Week: Monday.

Archangel Raphael (God's Doctor). Archangel Raphael is also called Israfel. Archangel Raphael is the Divine Spiritual Healer who stands before God's throne.

Archangel Raphael accompanied and protected Tobias on his journey to heal his father from blindness. Archangel Raphael provided protection and protected Tobias's future bride from the influence of evil.

Archangel Raphael is considered the patron of the conjugal love of young people, engaged couples, spouses, pharmacists, educators, travellers and refugees.

Pictures of Archangel Raphael show he is holding a jar containing medicaments and fish.

He is the patron of pharmacists, travellers and refugees. Archangel Raphael is God's Doctor and is the Archangel who can heal the soul, relieve suffering, and drive out demons.

Archangel Raphael is known as The Healing of God or the Medicine Doctor.

Archangel Raphael went to heal the injured of the Fallen Angels and demons.

Archangel Raphael is one of the principal characters in the deuterocanonical Book of Tobit.

Call upon Archangel Raphael for help with healing properties when you are not feeling well, feeling spiritually low, a little extra help in managing pain, travel assistance, and comforting and healing your pets.

Archangel Raphael offers his assistance and guidance to Medical Professions, Energy Healers and anyone who needs that little extra help.

Archangel Raphael's Cardinal Point is East.

"This does not mean that you should not go to your Doctor and not follow their guidance, always seek medical attention if needed."

Archangel Raphael's Mystical Traits:
Colours: Dark Pink, Emerald Green, and Green.
Crystal: Amethyst, Rose Quartz, Malachite, Epidote, Dioptase.
Chakra: Heart Chakra.
Element: Air.
Zodiac: Sagittarius, Leo, and Aries.
Planet: Mercury.
Day of the Week: Tuesday.

Archangel Uriel (The Fire of God, The Light of God).
Archangel Uriel is known as the Archangel, who holds the fiery sword that bars the gates to Eden. Archangel Uriel has other names as Sariel, Suriel, Muriel, Auriel, and Aretziel.

The difference in the Archangel's names is due to the Religious Faith you practice.

Archangel Uriel is the Archangel of Repentance and the Damned. Archangel Uriel is the Watcher over Hades. He is the patron of the Sacrament of Confirmation, the Archangel of salvation, and the healer of the planet.

The Reign of King Herod and the massacre of the innocents, John the Baptist, was rescued by Archangel Uriel. John the Baptist and his mother, Elizabeth, were guided to safety by Archangel Uriel. Archangel Uriel is the Archangel of intuition, insight, ideas and epiphanies which come suddenly.

People like artists of every kind, such as writers, musicians and painters, are intuitive and creative.

Whenever you have a mental block or do not know how to proceed with anything you are doing, you can call on Archangel Uriel for help.

Pray to Archangel Uriel and have him download the information you require for exams and overcome your creative blocks.

Archangel Uriel is the Archangel to call upon whenever a natural disaster strikes and to help smooth over the disagreeable times in your life, such as arguments and conflicts. Archangel Uriel is the Angel of devotion and in the service of receiving and giving.

Archangel Uriel's Cardinal Point is North.

Mystical Traits of Archangel Uriel
Colours: Gold, Purple, and Ruby Red.
Crystal: Obsidian, Pyrite, Tiger's Eye, Rutilated Quartz.
Chakra: Root Chakra and the Solar Plexus.
Element: Earth.
Zodiac: Libra, Gemini, and Aquarius.
Planet: Venus.
Day of the Week: Wednesday.

Archangel Raguel (Friend of God and the Secret of God). Archangel Raguel's other names are Raziel and Sealtiel. Archangel Raguel is the Archangel of Justice, Fairness, Harmony, Vengeance, Redemption, and Speech and the patron of the Sacrament of Holy Orders.

Archangel Raguel has a long history of fighting the injustice of sin caused by humans so they can live in harmony with God, and others while here on earth.

Archangel Raguel helps deliver some of the judgment of God. Archangel Raguel separates the faithful followers of God from others who have not followed God.

Archangel Raguel helps people by bringing guidance, wisdom, harmony, and peace into the lives who follow the teachings of God.

If you have personal problems in your home or work life, call Archangel Raguel to restore harmony.

Archangel Raguel will bring justice to the mistreated and motivate people to fight against crime.

The Mystical Traits of Raguel
Colour: Pale Blue, Scarlet and White.
Crystal: Aquamarine, Larimar, Amazonite, Fire Quartz, Ruby, and Mookaite.
Chakra: The Heart Chakra.
Element: Water.
Zodiac: Sagittarius.
Planet: Mars.
Day of the Week: Friday.

Archangel Phanuel (The Face of God). Archangel Phanuel is the Archangel of repentance and hope.

He is the Archangel who helps people to break free of sin, and helps people find hope when they turn to the hope that God can provide for them. You can pray to Archangel Phanuel when you need help, and you must turn away from sin and destruction.

Archangel Phanuel will lead you toward the faith of God and help you lead a life you will be proud to live.

These are some of the signs that you may be communicating with Phanuel.

You may feel the urge to repent any sin weighing you down.

Archangel Phanuel comes to you with a light blue ray of light.

Archangel Phanuel takes his directives under the guidance of Archangel Michael.

Archangel Phanuel's guidance comes with the hope that all is not lost. There is always a way for you to find a positive answer to your problem, and you will prevail. Having faith and igniting the power of hope with a deep sense of trust will help you overcome any obstacle you encounter.

Bright light may suddenly take over your surroundings. A sudden increase in light is always a good sign that Phanuel is nearby.

A golden ray of sunshine will lift your Spirit, knowing that all is well. It will fill you with all the warmth of good feelings of hope, your problems will turn out alright.

You will see the beauty around you, and your heart will be full of joy and peace.

Archangel Phanuel Mystical Traits
Colours: Blue.
Crystals: Angelite, Celestite, and Kyanite.
Chakra:
Element:
Zodiac:

Planet: Jupiter.
Day of the Week: Thursday.

Zerachiel, Sariel (God's Command) Zerachiel or Sariel, is the seventh Archangel, who has many names used throughout the centuries and different sects of Religion.

Archangel Zerachiel's other known names are Selaphiel, Salathiel, Selathiel, Seraphiel, Sarakiel, Saraqael, Zachariel, Baruchel and Sariel. Archangel Zerachiel is said to be one of the Watchers who watches over the ones who sin in Spirit.

Archangel Zerachiel is the Archangel of God's Judgment and the patron of the Sacrament of Matrimony.

Archangel Zerachiel Mystical Traits
Colours: Orange and Yellow.
Crystals: Orange Calcite, Creedite, and Sunstone.
Planet: Saturn.
Weekday: Saturday.

Note *** As I was researching the Archangels, there seems to be a difference in cultural beliefs depending in Global Religions. I noticed that some Religions have tried to match the Archangels to many different names, planets, zodiacs, numbers and crystals, which can be confusing. The old becomes new once again and is brought back into the light. Take what resonates with you and leave the rest.

There could be more than seven Archangels depending on the Religion and articles written on the subject.

Although the Catholic Church now recognizes other

Archangels, these Archangels will not be in the scriptures of the Bible.

If there are infinite numbers of angels, there certainly can be more Archangels to be named. Who is to say that it is not possible?

The research for this book came from many Religious Sources.

Guardian Angels

Do Guardian Angels Have Names?

All angels have names assigned to them by God upon their creation. Guardian Angels go by their names in the Heavenly Realm.

We do not have to call our Guardian Angels by their given names. The Angel will answer you regardless if you use their name or not. Since most of the population here on earth does not know our Guardian Angel's name, we can name them anything that is respectful.

You can always try to find your Guardian Angel's name by asking them their name. Then you use the first name that pops into your head.

The name you first thought of is usually the name of the Guardian Angel.

You can apply this method to find the names of other Spirits that come to visit.

You can ask your Guardian Angel's name in meditation.

Locate a quiet place where you will not be disturbed, and make yourself comfortable.

Relax, and clear your mind of all negative feelings and runaway thoughts.

Keep a controlled, uniform breathing pattern while you sit there to meditate.

Breath work will help to quieten that monkey mind that likes to jump from thought to thought.

94

Keep your mind clear of thoughts.

Ask your Guardian Angel their name.

Listen, and be aware of the first name that comes to you.

You may not hear your Guardian Angel's name right away.

You may have a strong gut instinct about what their name is.

Go with that name. It's a good chance that is your Guardian Angel's name.

Your Guardian Angel's name may be something you have never heard of before, or you cannot pronounce it.

In that case, give your Guardian Angel a name of your choosing. They will not care what you name them.

Another method you can do each morning is to ask your Guardian Angel to give you a letter of their name, and to give you letters of their name throughout the day.

Write down the letters that come to your mind.

If you do not get letters of their name throughout the day, you can ask your Guardian Angel for a letter each morning.

Write down each letter each morning until you have their full name.

Ask your Guardian Angel if the name you have written down is correct.

You can use guided meditations on YouTube to connect to your Guardian Angel.

Maybe in the meditation, you will see and be able to speak to your Guardian Angel. You must listen very carefully. You will hear the message telepathically.

After your meditation, remember to write everything you saw or heard down, so you will not forget.

This encounter with your Guardian Angel will be memorable for you.

Your Guardian Angel will appear to you in your dreams. You have to ask your Guardian Angel to visit you in your dreams.

When you wake in the morning, write down your dreams before your dreams fade away quickly, or before you think your dreams have no importance.

When you meet your Guardian Angel, it will be an experience you will not forget. The dream is so vivid and feels very different than all other dreams. Most people will not forget this experience. I know I never did.

Other people's Guardian Angels or Spirit Guides visited me in my dreams before that person said there was something wrong with them.

Show your Guardian Angel appreciation and gratitude. Say hello to them every morning and thank them for their presence and protection. Thank them when you have challenging times or near misses, or accidents. Sometimes your Guardian Angel will give you some intuitive thoughts to help you avoid mistakes. Everyone has these little hunches or gut feelings, even if they do not know how they came up with those thoughts.

Thank your Guardian Angel for constantly being with you and guiding you for your highest good and the highest good for all.

If you are doubtful that these interactions are not coming from your Guardian Angel, ask them to give you specific signs.

Signs from your Guardian Angel may start to appear unexpectedly in unexpected places. These signs may appear on billboards, when songs are playing on the radio, in books, or on television.

Ask your Guardian Angel to move something you know no one else would touch.

Your Guardian Angel or Spirit Guides will let you know they are nearby with a light touch to your shoulder, a little tickle on the back of your neck, or through other signs. Having sudden chills or you feel a little flush are other signs your Guardian Angel is nearby. Pay attention to these signs. Your Guardian Angel is trying to get your attention, provide help, and help protect you. They want to let you know they are near.

Guardian Angels are most commonly felt and detected by humans, and animals. They are little white orbs. They travel within groups of other angels, who you will need at that particular time to fulfill that part of your sacred contract. Guardian Angels will appear to a person to remind them that they are never alone. They come to you with encouragement, and to let you know you are loved and cared for by them. They bring inspiration and to have faith when you are going through challenging circumstances. They do not carry complex messages. They will not impose themselves into your life unless you ask them for help. Guardian Angels are simply there to be of service and bestow their blessings on you.

Angels

What are Angels?

Angels are spiritual entities of the Angelic Hierarchy and the Heavenly Choir. These spiritual entities of Angels are messengers from God or your Higher Source. The Angels come to earth to work with humans in their time of need. Angels have no Religious Affiliation, regardless of how many faiths are practiced here on earth.

Angels will always be there. They are like your best friend, all you have to do, is call on them for help. Angels can lead you in the right direction without you even knowing it.

Angels are Orbs of electromagnetic energy that contain shining sparks of energy particles. These bright lights will manifest into balls known as Orbs. Orbs of light will appear in various colours depending on the type of Angel.

People reported Orbs, shafts of light, or rays of light have appeared suddenly on the earthly realm close to where people were. Angel orbs are more complex than simple specks of light. Orbs are patterns of geometric shapes.

The colour of the Angel's orb defines which group the Angel belongs to. Every Angel has a distinct colour. The colours help to distinguish what type of Angel came to visit you. Angels often travel in groups. Each Angel is assigned a specific task that they can perform to help you when there is a need.

Before birth, you and your Angels planned what your life would be like here on earth. That plan contains which type of Angel and the time they would come to assist you. Angels will not intervene in your life until you ask them for help. The Angel will intervene if it is to prevent you from doing something that alters your life plan drastically.

There is a lot of misconception about Angels. We will not and cannot become Angels when we pass on to the Other Side. It is not because a person is not worthy enough or we have not lived a life of purity. We can be generous and compassionate and lead reverent lives to warrant a divine life. God will never find us unworthy. Angels and humans are physiologically two different species.

We cannot gaze or look upon an Angel for very long because the composition of an Angel is fire. The illuminating glow of the Angel is too intense, and it would hurt our eyes. Angels will never incarnate because they have never lived a life on earth.

Angels can take on a human form to complete their mission on earth. There are millions of stories of earthly encounters with Angels helping people in a crisis. People who have seen Angels remarked on their exquisite features and glistening skin tones in every human race. Angels are illuminating white light which comes from within.

Angels are Incorporeal.

The description of Incorporeal means (Angels lacking in material form or substance.)

Angels are orbs of electromagnetic energy field which contain geometric shapes of Angelic energy. Angels are invisible most of the time. Angels cannot present themselves physically for very long because it would take too much energy for an Angel to maintain a physical body. Angels are androgynous. Angels can take the form of either female or male. When Angels have to make an appearance, they will wear the same clothes as the culture of the person who needs help. The Angels will speak to you in the language you are accustomed to. Angels will make appearances with or without their wings.

Sometimes Angels will make an appearance in their garments, and if they do, they will have a blinding light surrounding them. You will not be able to see what they are wearing or the gender of the Angel. Angels are obedient and perform God's will, and as it is said, Angels have moral judgment. These Divine Beings have an infinite life to serve God because they are immortal and cannot die.

Angels have personal free will and have emotional feelings, such as happiness or sadness, and they are intelligent. Your Angels and Guardian Angels have the same emotions as you, but they will not intervene because you came to this planet to learn all you can to complete your mission, before you return to Heaven.

Angels can appear in one place at a time. Angels are Spiritual remarkable beings of God's creations, and they will show up when someone is in need without you knowing who they are. No one knows how many Angels are in the Universe. They are too numerous to assign a number.

Angels will show up in a physical body and help you, then disappear as fast as they came. Angels will talk to you telepathically and save their voices to sing praises of worship to God. Angels can communicate through our thoughts, dreams, lines in a song, and through conversations with others, such as strangers and friends talking on the street.

Angels can come to us in our dreams to communicate with us and to keep us on our Spiritual path. From the time of your birth until your death, your Guardian Angels will always be there to support you.

Angel orbs travel through the Universe at higher vibrational frequencies, faster than any person can perceive in our natural field of vision.

When angels approach people or a person, they slow the rate of speed they are travelling at considerably, then the Orb of an Angel may be detected by a human. The person catches a glimpse of an angel or sees the Orb of an Angel, or maybe it is a shaft of light.

You sense you are not alone, even when you are in the company of others. The feeling one gets is something different about the atmosphere around them. That sense of knowing something is off. At these times, an uneasy feeling comes over you that someone is watching you. Angelic Being and Ancestral Spirits are most likely in your presence.

Angels are Spiritual entities of an Angelic Hierarchy. The Heavenly Hierarchy of Angels has different levels or categories under which an Angel may fall. It does not matter what level of an Angel. All Angels are of one rank. No angel is any more special than another Angel.

There are many categories of Angels because each Angel will specialize in their field of expertise. When looking at Angels and their grouping, you would think they would have a ranking system. Angels are spiritual entities that come in many shapes and forms. They are Guides and Messengers from God.

The Different Colours of Angel Orbs and their Meanings.

The Seven Colours of Orbs Seen by Humans:

Blue Orbs - Power, protection, faith, courage, and strength.
Yellow Orbs - Wisdom in decisions.

Pink Orbs - Love, Peace, and Tranquility.
White Orbs - Purity, Harmony, and Holiness.
Green Orbs - Healing and Prosperity.
Red Orbs - Wise Service.
Purple Orbs - Mercy and Transformation.

Angelic Light Rays More Than the Seven Colours.

Silver Orbs - A spiritual message.
Gold Orbs - Unconditional love.
Black Orbs - Evil.
Brown Orbs - Danger.
Orange Orbs - Forgiveness.

There are eight levels for Angels.

Angels are considered all equal, but Angels can and will progress to a higher level. The highest Choir of Angels is the Seraphim, Cherubim, and Thrones, the closest to God.

The Category of Angels and the colours of their wings are listed below.

Seraphim have white wings with silver tips.
Cherubim have white wings with gold tips.
Thrones have deep purple wings.
Dominions have green wings.
Virtues have pale blue wings.
Powers
Principalities have solid gold wings.
Archangels have pure white wings.
Angels have dusty gray-white wings.

The First Seven Levels of Angels Will Intervene to Help in a Crisis:

Principalities:

The Principalities will only go where God has instructed, as to his command. The Principalities can create miracles, prevent fatalities and turn around the most misguided lives of people.

Principalities are also known as the Rulers and governors of the Astral World between Heaven and Earth. They guide and protect nations or groups of people like institutions such as churches. They take charge of all other angels and instruct them to fulfill the divine ministry. They are the angels of birth and death. Their celestial form is the form of shimmering hazy bright lights. Their purpose is to overthrow the demons who roam in the Astral Realm.

Principalities have solid gold wings.

Seraphim:

Seraphim Angels fly high above God. Seraphim are so near God that they appear to be burning. They even have to protect themselves from the brilliance of God's presence, and no evil or harm can penetrate the armour of a Seraphim.

Seraphim (The burning ones) has six wings and the continual cry of Holy, Holy, Holy. One set of wings covered their faces in reverence, the second set covered their feet in humility, and the center set of wings is for when they move back and forth, and when they fly. The Seraphim Angels sit close to the throne of God. They are closer to God than any Holy Spirit.

The Seraphim are the highest-ranking group in the Choirs of Heaven. Seraphim have white wings with silver tips.

Cherubim

The word Cherubim means to be diligent. The Cherubim are the Angels that stand close to God's throne. Cherubim are the short pudgy naked valentine babies often thought of as Cherubs, and they have some resemblance to man. The Cherubim are the Angels with flaming swords that bar the entrance to Eden.

Under the Cherubim wings, there is the shape of a man's hand, and there are four wheels under each Cherub. The wheels gleamed of a tarnished stone the wheels are inside the wheels. The wheels can move in all four directions without turning their body or head. The body and wings of the Cherubim are full of eyes. Each Cherubim has four faces. The first face of a Cherub is a bull or ox, the second the face of a man, the third face of a lion, and the fourth face of an eagle. They appear to have human hands and are living Creatures of fiery. The Cherubim sit at the right side of the temple, with a cloud filled with the inner court of Heaven. They have four wings and four faces. The Cherubim are assigned special duties of guarding the entrance to Eden after Adam and Eve's fall from grace. God instructed that two golden Cherubs are to set on the Ark of the Covenant. The Cherubs are to be facing each other at opposite ends.

Cherubim have white wings with gold tips.

Thrones:

Thrones are the angels that protect all the planets in the cosmos, and anything of physical matter begins to take shape. The Thrones are of pure humility, peace and submission. The Thrones are known to have the power of judgment and act as counsellors to the angels and aid them. The Thrones are the keeper of celestial records that hold God's knowledge. Thrones can be sent to earth to perform great tasks.

The Thrones have purple wings.

Dominions:

Dominions are the Lordships, Lords, and the angels of creation. They concern themselves with the order of the Universe. Dominions direct the lower spheres of angels to ensure and keep order in the Universe. All who serve God are fit to be rulers. Obedience is the predominant factor in all we do. Dominions resemble beautiful humans with a set of wings. Their swords or sceptres have light orbs at the top to distinguish them from other angels. The Dominions are the heavenly ones who are the governors, and they strike a balance between Spirit and matter, good or bad.

Dominions have green wings.

Virtues:

Virtues are known for their grace and bestowing blessings of God's miracles. Virtues are known as the Strongholds, the shining ones, and the worker bees. God sent the Virtues to earth to bring power to the heads of government and other authority figureheads. The Virtues supervise the movement of angels to ensure that the cosmos remain in order. The Virtues have the unshaken fortitude to serve God. Virtues are the spirits of motion and control the elements, as the seasons on earth and all planetary objects in the cosmos. The Virtues provide courage, valour for heroism and grace. Virtues aid in the struggle between good and evil. You can call upon the Virtues in times of sickness and accidents.

The Virtues have pale blue wings.

Powers:

The Powers are the warrior Angels that fight against evil spirits and defend the cosmos and humans.

The Powers are sparks of light. The Powers oversee maintaining the order of the natural world. They inspire all living things, even in the scientific community. The Powers take orders from the angels above and convert them into miracles for the deserving. When Powers make themselves known here on earth, they present themselves in the earthly form of musicians, artists, healers, and scientists who work with the power of love and physics.

Archangels:

Archangels are angels of one of the highest sources of God. They are rays of light that can appear as light shafts whispering in your ears or Orbs of light. The archangels are the watchers of all God's creations. They stand by to nudge and to guide us in the right direction. They can be a source of comfort when it is needed. They may even be the little voice in your ear or talking in your mind reminding you. You are never alone, and help is always available. Archangels are not always by your side. Archangels oversee all the other angels and spirit guides, nations, Religion, politics, and all matters of humankind. Archangels can change their physical form to help innovators, philosophers, nation leaders and human rights leaders. They change into human form to help people when faced with a crisis. Many people reported that angelic beings helped them when they were in grave danger. An angel can appear instantaneously and disappear just as fast after human help has arrived.

Whenever I see a blue orb or blue shaft of light, I always think of Archangel Michael. I can be going about my day, and when I feel I am not alone, I sense someone is looking at me. I suddenly look up. I see a tall figure of blue haze standing in my dining room. After seeing this blue haze, I see blue all the time, even when my eyes are closed. It only happens for a couple of days then it fades away.

Guardian Angels and Angels

Guardian Angels were assigned to everyone before we departed from the Other Side. Our Guardian Angel will guide us through the most trying times in our lives. They can call in other angels who specialize in specific fields.

I have been with people in their last remaining hours on earth when they were coming out of one of their naps. The person remarked they were in Heaven looking at all the glorious sights. These people have heard the magnificent singing of the Angels praising God. The Angels were known to sing one time on earth. It was when they sang at the time of Jesus Christ's birth.

Sometimes Angels will help to escort a person to the other side when they have a Near Death Experience. Then the person is to return to earth with a mission and to tell the world that there is life after death.

Spirit Guides

Everyone has at least one Spirit Guide. A Spirit Guide is a spiritual being from the Kingdom of Heaven.

A Spirit Guide is a form of energy that will sometimes appear like an energy ball or an orb to humans here on earth. A Spirit Guide will help you when needed. They are like that little inner voice you hear in your mind. Sometimes when you are trying to make a decision, that little voice of your inner self will tell you to go for it or not do it. Everyone knows that feeling. A Spirit Guide is only here to help keep you on the right track so you can fulfill your objectives for your sacred contract.

Lack of belief does not bother them. They will still give you that nudge to achieve your purpose. A Spirit Guide will not impose its will on you.

You still have your free will. It is up to you how you use it.

If you need help, all you have to do is call on your Spirit Guide for guidance. They will gladly guide you to what you need. Not for what you want. The two are different. What you want may not be for your highest good, and you may not receive what you want.

If you ask for what you need and if it is for your highest good and the highest good of all, you may get what you need. So, in other words, wishes are not granted.

There are many different Spirit Guides. A Spirit Guide specializes in their field of expertise.

The Roles of Spirit Guides

The roles of your Spirit Guides are to help you live your life purpose as to what you planned in your sacred contract. That is the plan you made before you left the Spiritual World before this reincarnation. Spirit Guides, make sure you do not deviate from your plotted course. They are to help protect you from harm, negativity and evil. Spirit Guides will be the source of your inspiration. They will help you to use your innate gifts.

Ancestral Spirit Guides

Yes, you can have Ancestors as Spirit Guides. We all do. Spirit Guides can be from many prior centuries. Some of these Ancestral Guides are not for our highest good. We have to be wary of their savoury traits. Or things they want us to do out of character. Ancestral family members may have agendas they want us to follow. We cannot become one of their victims. They may try to guide us by limiting our beliefs and projecting trauma and generational fears into our subconscious. Past traumas and fears from ancestors play a part in our everyday life. These ancestral inflictions need to heal before we move on Spiritually.

Some Ancestral Spirit Guides are inspirational teachers, and they provide us with their knowledge of things we have had no prior knowledge of, and help us develop our gifts. Other Ancestral Spirit Guides are the ones no one wants to listen to, they are not here to help for our highest good, and the highest good for all. They are spirits connected to you through your spiritual or genetic lineage. You may need to connect to your ancestral relatives to heal the limiting beliefs, generational fears, wounds and trauma.

Some of these Ancestor Spirit Guides can help you heal emotionally and physically. They can help remove obstacles that seem to have reoccurring themes in your life. Ancestral Spirit Guides can provide insight when you meditate. Beware, not all Spirits who come through when you meditate are there to help you for your highest good and the good of humanity.

Your Ancestors will contact you through your dreams. It is easier for them to connect with you when you are sleeping. Your subconscious is more relaxed and receptive to hearing what they may have to say. Some people will build an Ancestral Altar to honour their Ancestors. They believe that the altar and their intentions will bring their ancestors closer to them.

Ascended Masters

Ascended Masters are a part of the Spirit Guide Realm. They are the Spirits of people who have lived on earth and ascended Spiritually to the highest enlightenment.

They have chosen to be Spirit Guides to help people enlighten and achieve their highest good spiritually. They guide people with wise knowledge of their expertise and keep you on track with your sacred plan. Ascended Masters are not on the karmic cycle of reincarnation.

You can channel your Master Guides through automatic writing, lucid dreams, Astral Projection, Astral Travel, and Meditation.

Ascension Spirit Guides

Ascension Spirit Guides will help you ascend to the next spiritual level, and on to the next level. They keep you on track to following your sacred plan of ascension into the spiritual realm.

Astral Guides

Astral Guides help you travel periodically from earth to other Astral and heavenly realms. Your Astral Guides will show your Spirit how you can leave your body safely, and return to it anytime you wish when you are asleep.

Astral Projection Guides

Astral Projection Guides will help and teach you how to Astral Project safely. Astral Projection happens when you are awake. For a brief time, your Spirit will leave your body. Your Spirit will travel remotely to another destination and take in all the sights.

Body Spirit Guides

Body Spirit Guides help you to protect your body from emotional, spiritual and physical harm.

Elemental Spirit Guides

Elemental Spirit Guides are the fairies, elves or pixies of the metaphysical world. These Elementals are the wonders of the magical world of Fairy Tales.

There are four different types of Elementals.

The classic elementals are the earth, fire, air and water.

Gnomes are elementals associated with the earth. Mermaids and undines are spirit elementals that associate with water. Salamanders are an elemental that associate with fire, and sylphs are air elementals spirits without souls. Sylphs can take on shapes in the air as clouds and light forms. There is a fifth elemental, and they are spirits with human souls.

Are these imaginary creatures of fairy tales? I do not think they are all imaginary, especially what we call fairies.

I have seen a real live fairy. She was tiny and beautiful. My husband and I were walking one day, and I looked down. In the taller grass, I saw this little fairy. She was as surprised as I was, when we saw each other. I shook my head and looked again, I even started moving the grass around to have a second look, but I did not find her. I asked my husband if he had seen her, and he said he did not see her.

The elements are associated with the spirits of nature. They can appear in human form and help people with challenges, make minor changes like making it rain, and have the sun shine brighter. They can grant wishes, especially in love and luck.

I know. I was too surprised at seeing her to make a wish. I was trying to make sense of what I saw. I was in awe. I will not forget my glorious encounter with a fairy.

Helper Spirit Guides

Helper Spirit Guides are not always with you. They will come and go as needed. Helper guides continuously change when you need help. You will get another helper guide when it is time for you to learn a new skill. These guides change for more knowledgeable guides.

Joy Spirit Guides

Joy Spirit Guides help by trying to keep the joy in your heart and life. They do this by reminding you of your child playfulness and bringing you back to more joyful times in your life.

Karmic Spirit Guides

Karmic Spirit Guides will help you work through collective karma from past lives, and your karma now in this lifetime. They will help you shed the chains that hold you back, so you can move to the next level of your soul purpose.

Life Spirit Guides

Life Spirit Guides are in charge of all the Spirit Guides. Life Guides are instrumental roles when planning our life plan, also known as our sacred contract.

Life Guides help plan our birth, and the life we plan to live until our death. Life Spirit Guides co-operate with all other spirit guides. These Life guides are also known as Guardian Angels.

Timing Spirit Guides

Timing Spirit Guides handle all synchronizations of our life. They make sure we are in the right place at the right time. The places we go, the events that happen in our lives and the people we meet have all been preplanned in our sacred contract. Nothing is left to chance.

Teaching Spirit Guides

Our teaching guides teach us all the life lessons in our lesson plan, and see that we are developing physically, and spiritually through our meditations and dreams.

They will leave signs for you to follow and keep on track. When you stray off your planned path, your Teaching Guides will nudge you, and get you back on your predetermined life path.

Creativity Spiritual Guides

Creative Spirit Guides will help you with your creative side and inspire you while you work.

They can connect with you through your dreams and connect you with your inner thoughts and talent. They will reveal to you what you need to know. It is always good to keep your eyes open and try something new.

Animal Spirit Guides

Animal Spirit Guides are part of the belief of many spiritual cultures. Some of these cultures are Paganism, Wicca and Native American.

People have Animal Spirit Guides. Many people are unaware they have animals for Spirit Guides because the animal's work is so subtle. Some people can sense an animal watching over them or sitting near by. They are there for your protection. People have a natural attraction to an animal and do not know why. That animal can be anything unusual, and it can even be an elephant. How many people would think of having an elephant as a Spirit Guide, Totem, or pet in the western world? These Spirit Guides can be any animal or insect known to our world.

I think my Spirit Animal Guide is a black panther. I have had incidents where I could have sworn that there was a big black panther in my house. This animal likes to climb into bed with me, especially when I am alone at night.

It will sit at the bottom of my bed or lay close to my lower legs. I know this animal is there. I feel its weight and its large stature body next to me. I have seen a black panther sitting in my hallway. This hallway is between the front and back doors of my house.

Star Beings and Starseed Souls

Star beings are extraterrestrials of our galactic family. The Star Beings are from many different galaxies of the universe. The Star Beings work to help maintain well-being and compassion for all humanity.

These Starseed Souls are from higher dimensional life from other star systems.

Some star systems you may have heard of are Lyra, Andromeda, Sirius, and Pleiades.

Pleiadians, Sirians, Arcturians, Andromedans, Orians, Lemurians, Atlanteans, and Lyrans are extraterrestrials with a collective consciousness. People channel these Star Beings for their consciousness of higher ascension for Spiritual Enlightenment.

Protection Guides

Protection Guides are Spirit Guides that are very much as their name refers to them. They are essentially our protectors. They act as our bodyguards to keep harm, negativity and evil away as much as permitted. Remember, we have the free will to make our own choices and what kind of entities we let influence our lives.

Signs Your Spirit Guides are Around You

There are many signs you may get from your Spirit Guides. These signs are very subtle, and you can miss them or never give them a second thought. You may feel you have a spiritual tug of war trying to keep on your chosen path. Influences from others may not be for your greatest good.

You may get sudden waves of emotions. Sometimes you may experience sudden happiness, waves of sadness for no reason, or you get a feeling of great inner peace that all is well with the world. These can be signs that your Spirit Guides are near you.

You may suddenly get a heavy feeling or sudden chest pain which goes away as suddenly. These are signs of your Spirit Guides trying to get your attention. If you get these feelings, they want you to slow down and pay attention to yourself and your surroundings. Strong feelings felt in your Solar Plexuses are what we call gut feelings. When you experience these feelings, try to recall what you were thinking and doing.

Goosebumps, tingling and the feeling of being touched are common signs your Spirit Guides are right there with you.

Ringing in your ears is another sign your Spirit Guides are downloading information for you to access later.

Synchronism is another sign your Spirit Guides are close by. You may see things on billboards that have meaning to you. Seeing Angel Numbers just about anywhere on digital clocks or license plates, or you are thinking about someone, and they call or appear out of the blue is one of the mysteries of synchronism. Spirit Guides will give you signs through other people by doing things to them, like softly touching them. Your friend suddenly starts talking to you about subjects you are interested in, and you know they did not have a prior interest in that subject.

Contacting Your Spirit Guides

Everyone has a team of Spirit Guides. Your Guides have been with you since before you left the Other Side. They helped you plan your sacred chart before this incarnation to earth. Your Guides came to earth with you. They are here to help you learn and fulfill your objectives before you return to the Other Side. Your Guides stayed with you throughout your birth. They will never leave you while you are on this planet. Your Guides and you will return to the Other Side when you leave earth. Once you have completed what you came here to learn.

Your Spirit Guides stay within proximity of you. Many people can sense the presence of their Spirit Guides. They feel there is someone or something near them, or you catch a quick glimpse out of the corner of your eye and then it is gone. Your Spirit Guides are here to help you in not an intrusive way.

They will talk to you telepathically without you knowing it is them. They will give you advice, and you have the free will to choose whatever you decide. This debate will go on inside your mind as if you have made the decision yourself. You know what I mean. Let's say you have an opportunity for a new job, and you have to decide if the new job will be beneficial for you, and for you to take a new position. Your Guides will help you to weigh the pros and cons.

You make the decision yourself. Other times, you may hear your conscience screaming not to do something, and you do otherwise. The outcome is not what you expected. It was your decision, and you have to live with the consequences.

Your Spirit Guides will leave you subtle signs which may not be easy to pick up on. Pay attention to all the signs you receive. The signs are subtle and never too small. If you have trouble picking up on these signs and anything unusual happens, write it down in a journal.

If you think someone is speaking to you, pay attention and listen, it is probably one of your Spirit Guides or a loved one who has passed on.

If you have a disease or mental issues or hear voices in your head all the time, get medical help, or take your medication, it is probably not your Spirit Guides speaking to you.

You must ask God and the Holy Spirit for protection first. You do not want to encourage other Spirits who might be hanging around. Some Spirits may be friendly, and some Spirits may be dark entities looking for a way to influence you. If you need help, you can ask your Spirit Guides for assistance.

To ask your Spirit Guides for help, and by praying. Or you can say a simple prayer like the one I use frequently.

"Lord, please surround me with the White Light of the Holy Spirit, and the Light of God's divine protection to help protect me, and show me the way to shine the light. I ask this in Jesus's name."

Or you can make up your version.

After you have asked for protection, you meditate and visualize the White Light of the Holy Spirit surrounding you. Once you see the White Light, call your Spirit Guides to help you with whatever help you need. You will be amazed at how much easier it is to do whatever you have to do.

Remember, your Spirit Guides are here to assist you when you need help. All you have to do is ask.

There is one meditation I like to do. I find it relaxing before I go to sleep for the night.

I think of the tranquillity of being on a sandy beach somewhere in the Caribbean. I am sitting on the sand, looking out at the clear blue water of the ocean.

I am enjoying the cool soothing tropical breeze. The breeze is gently swaying the palm trees on this beautiful island. A bent palm tree is a convenient bench where people can sit. On this bench sits a man. This man is my Spirit Guide.

Sometimes we communicate not with words but telepathically. We are the only two people on this beach. I have a comforting feeling knowing he is there.

At times, I have found solutions for some problems I have been pondering. You can quietly sit by yourself. When your mind is calm, call out to summon your Spirit Guide. Ask him. "What is your name?" Take the first name that pops into your mind. That name is most likely the name of your Spirit Guide. You have many Spirit Guides. It is not uncommon to come up with a few different names.

Ask your Spirit Guide who they are. From where they came? You can ask them to give you an answer to a private question, the answer is one that you would only know.

There are so many ways to communicate with your Spirit Guide. You do it all the time. You only have to recognize the signs. Try to communicate with them intentionally.

You may be surprised by how easy it is to call upon your Spirit Guide for help, or maybe have a little chat. Many people do it all the time, so why not you?

Angel Numbers

Angels are Divine Beings who have walked the earth since the beginning of time.

When I was a child, I saw Angels when I was very sick in the hospital.

Many believe that Angels come from Heaven. Many do not believe in Angels, and that is their right. They are not paying attention to the subtle signs the Angels are leaving.

The signs Angels leave come in many ways, and one of the signs can show a sequence of numbers appearing in random places. Random numbers on license plates, billboards, and sales receipts have sequential numbers you can use as Angel Numbers. You hear a song on the radio that reminds you of a person or a time in your life. Watching movies on Television can trigger a memory that can be an Angel Sign.

The Greek Philosopher Pythagoras believed numbers had a vibrational frequency that corresponded to those of musical notes. Mr. Pythagoras devised a system using the vibrational frequency of numbers to interpret the meaning of people's names, and birth dates and place of birth. Matching the letters to numbers is often used in Numerology. Astrologers use the month, date, and year of birth to find the person's astrological sign.

This system is known as Pythagorean Numerology.

Modern-day Numerology focuses on the values of your name to provide your destiny number. Your date of birth will focus on your life path number. These numbers provide the character traits of your personality and show you where the challenges are within your life path.

Angel Numbers, Angel Numbers Key Codex, and Numerology combined with a spiritual perspective are how your Soul and Angels will leave signs to guide you towards your Soul's path for this lifetime.

Angel Numbers Key Codex

0. It is the time for new beginnings. Doors are opening for you now. God is near you now.

1. **The Self, Oneness, Higher Self, Universal Connection.**
2. **Union, Connection to Others, Aligning with Love.**
3. **Expansion, Higher Power, The Masters.**
4. **Angels, Communication, Gifts Expanding.**
5. **Changes, Effort, Action, and input required.**
6. **Balance, Intention Required, Carefulness.**
7. **Magic, Manifestation, Divine Inspiration.**
8. **Journey, Growth, Spiritual Lessons.**
9. **Self-mastery, Union with Higher-Self, Divine Feminine.**

Note: When using a digital clock, refer to the Angel Number Key Codex Chart.

This information is found in Angel Numbers by Kyle Gray. Kyle Gray is known as the man who speaks to Angels. Kyle Gray lives in the southern part of Scotland. Kyle Gray is just one of many who channels Angels to gain information from them.

What are Angel Numbers?

Angel Numbers are numbers that appear in patterns. The number patterns are sequences of three or four-like numbers that are together. For example, a person may see 222 or 2222. When you see double or triple number patterns, these are signs of Angel numbers. These are signs, your Angels send to get your attention. Number sequences reveal your energetic vibration frequency at that specific time, and how your life path is unfolding before you.

Ascending Numbers:

There can be a progression of numbers that some people call the ladder numbers. These numbers have a pattern of ascending.

For example, these numbers may show up as 12:34, and when you see these numbers like this, it means that you are going in the right direction on your life path. You are moving up to a higher level of consciousness.

Numbers like 123 mean that you are going in the right direction and moving to another step of higher consciousness.

Descending Numbers:

When you see descending numbers 4,3,2,1 like this, stop what you are doing, and take the time to reflect on what is holding you back.

Angel Numbers and Their Meaning:

000 or 0000. Seeing a sequence of zeros is a good indication of a fresh start. You are at the beginning of a new stage of your life, be ready to move on and take the necessary steps to help you grow.

111 or 1111. Your angels are trying to get your attention and confirm you are on the right path. Your intentions are manifesting. Make sure you are focusing on what is important to you.

Number ones can be desired numbers people make their wishes

on when they see a sequence of ones. Your Angels are in your presence now. You have the support of the Angels, your Spirit Guides, and your Ancestors. Your dreams and hopes can manifest, so be careful what you wish. You may get something you do not want.

According to Numerology when seeing ones can help bring energy into existence. You are one you are encouraged to use thoughts and intentions positively.

222 or 2222. A series of two's mean you are in alignment and balance. You are receiving help from someone in the physical or Spiritual Realm. The Angels are guiding you to reach your goals, and this is an excellent time to reach out for help, whether from a trusted friend or a Divine Spirit. Have trust and faith in yourself, and do not let stress and negativity come between you and your connection to the spiritual Realm. Let your Angels handle your worries, negative thoughts and fears. You have the influential energy of an earth angel, and you have a positive influence on people. You make people feel comfortable and safe.

333 or 3333. A sequence of threes is a sign from your Angels prompting you to stop procrastinating and let the creativity flow through you.

Get moving, and meditate to seek balance in your life. Lean into your innate gifts, and bring your talents and abilities into a situation. Doing so will bring abundance and more value to whatever you are navigating. Your Angels and Ascending Masters are right there with you and guiding you. You are in great hands and surrender into their hands. 3's are the Master numbers of teachers in Numerology, and they carry messages, and challenges to overcome fears. Take chances and embrace the challenges coming your way. Do not be afraid your Angels will take you to the finish line.

444 or 4444. Your Angels and Spirit Guides hear your prayers and requests when you have a sequence of number fours. Your Angels and Spirit Guides are there to help and protect you. When you are facing challenges at this time, rest assured your guardians are leading you into the light. Do not be afraid to ask for help or assistance when navigating long-term projects or problems in your life.

Have faith in yourself. Establishing trust will bring you to new heights. Your angels are protecting you. Angels surround you as they lead you into the light. The angels are reminding you to take some time for yourself. You need time to help you regain your balance. You have been working hard. You need to relax and spend time with the people you care for and love.

555 or 5555. A sequence of fives indicates that changes are in the works for the better. The people who are involved in the decision-making are weighing all sides.

Change is not bad, but it can be frightening. Change is good for you and leads you to a better life. Your Angels and Guides reaffirm you are on the right path. Have faith. Things are about to get exciting. Trust your intuition, especially when you hear your little voice is encouraging you to go in another direction.

666 or 6666. A sequence of sixes is not to be feared. It is not demonic. Six is supportive, empathetic, and compassionate. Six are reminders that you should be kinder to yourself and treat yourself with understanding and compassion. Do not be so critical of yourself.

Things do not always go as you planned. Go with the flow. Everything happens for a reason. Take responsibility for your life and change what you think needs addressing. Reconnect with your Spirituality. Sixes can be a word of caution. Pay close attention to the people around you, and be careful when giving out your personal information. All people are not to be trusted. Do not reveal too much about yourself.

777 or 7777. Sevens are fortunate to have. Sevens bring an abundance of good luck. Sevens denote wise financial decisions, and a windfall may be in the works. New opportunities are on the way, with many possibilities to explore, maybe out of your comfort zone.

Let go of your fears and relax. You are in good hands with your Angels and Guides. Live and embrace the present, and trust everything will turn out fine. You are on your Spiritual path. Wishes and dreams have a way of coming true. Be careful what you wish for, and be sure it is something you want or need.

888 or 8888. Eights have Spiritual connections to the Spirit Realm. People who believe in the afterlife may see eights everywhere. These people connect to the Spiritual Realm by receiving messages from the supernatural. Eights have the support of their ancestors who passed before them. Number eight represents the infinity sign, an endless loop of a person's lifetime and energy. Dive deep into your intuition to receive support from your Ancestors, Spirit Guides and Guardian Angels. Eights can also represent money coming to that person and can be a sign of financial stability. Angels are encouraging you to break away from negative repeating patterns that are preventing you from moving forward.

Relationships and unfulfilled work fall into this category.

999 or 9999. Nines, mean you are completing a project or phase of your life. You are ready to move on to your next endeavours. Nines bring good news. Start a new beginning that is meaningful to you. Step out of your comfort zone, be brave, explore all the new possibilities, expand your horizons, and have fun. Go back to school

or start a new career. Angels hear your prayers and answer them from Heaven.

Your angels are working around you and providing you with strength. Have faith in yourself, and you can succeed in whatever you want to accomplish in this life.

1010. This number has a personal and a business meaning. The business and career meanings are for you to watch for new opportunities. Take action and pay attention to the signs. In your personal life, the angels will guide you to all the good things, including helping you find love. The message is not to give up and settle for the wrong person. The right person is yet to come along. That person may be right by your side, and you both have yet to realize you belong together.

Chapter Three

Recognizing Energy

Recognizing energy is easy to do all you have to do is have an open mind. Most of the population are skeptics. The skeptics have a difficult time acknowledging anything they cannot see.

Listen to your little inner voice, and trust your intuition. Without stepping out of your comfort zone and trusting your intuition, you are turning yourself off to the amazing things the world has to offer.

You are sitting at home watching television when you feel a slight cool breeze, and you know there is no reason for the temperature change. The temperature change is not affecting the rest of the room, only where you are sitting. This feeling does not last long. Your little hairs on your body stand up, and you have goosebumps. Why? One of your departed loved ones came to visit you. Maybe it is an Angelic Spirit.

Often people will get little glimpses, quick flashes of something, and they do not know what it could have been. It could have been an Archangel, Guardian Angel, Spirit Guide or a departed loved one.

An Angelic Spirit will appear as little orbs of light or a shaft of light. They will not materialize unless they have to intervene.

A person may have lost hope. They needed reassurance there was a God, a Higher Source, or a Divine Being of their faith. Maybe you're stranded somewhere and need help. An angel may make a brief appearance until your crisis is over. The Angel will stay until help has arrived. Then the Angel will disappear as fast as it had appeared.

Many people have told countless stories of the kind stranger who had stopped to help, and they are nowhere in sight when they turn to thank them for their help. Sometimes no other person has seen this person who assisted the one in need. Angels or Guardian Angels were intervening on your behalf.

You are going about your day, and you have your departed loved one on your mind, and your thoughts of them are persistent. That is when your departed loved one is by your side, enjoying your company and trying to get your attention. Your thoughts and conversations in your mind, of your departed loved ones, are not in your imagination. You are having that conversation with them.

Many people have found pennies, feathers, or something that feels different, and they cannot figure out what it is. That is when the Spiritual world is trying to make contact with you. All you have to do is acknowledge the signs. The Spirits in the Spiritual world find it difficult to materialize in this dense atmosphere of our world. Spirits do not have a physical body. It takes too much energy for them to appear in a physical form as we know them.

That is why we can only catch glimpses of shadow, orbs or shafts of light when they visit us. We may not be able to see them, but we can certainly feel them. You know that feeling. The feeling we are not alone when no one is with us.

If you do not believe, you will not be able to see or sense energy. When you have faith, you can do anything, and you do it. It is no different in the Spiritual World. You have to believe that there is a Spiritual World, and the Spiritual World is living with us in our material world. Your belief is the power of your intentions and knowing you can manifest what you need to do daily to achieve your goals. If you do not believe in Spiritual energy, you will not be able to make contact with departed loved ones or see what is beyond our material world.

Many people have changed their minds and started speaking about their Near-Death Experiences. They are coming forward or making YouTube Videos and speaking as a guest on Podcasts about their Near-Death Experiences. They are no longer afraid to talk about their NDEs because they know that they are not the only one who has experienced this phenomenon. The fear has subsided in people not believing them. Telling their stories of their journey to Heaven and back is therapeutic for them. When they visited the other side of the veil, their loved ones were there to greet them. They told the person having the NDE they had to return to their body, and it was not their time to leave this world.

They had a mission to complete, and they must return to earth to spread the word that there is a Spiritual life after death, and there is a Heaven and a Divine Higher Source or God.

You use your imagination to work on everything you accomplish daily. You used your imagination to plan your future. People make vision boards, a map of manifesting their future selves and life. Your knowledge and understanding are limited, your imagination is limitless, and you can embrace the entire world with belief.

Einstein said it best. "Imagination is more important than knowledge. Knowledge is a limit to all we know and understand, while imagination embraces the entire world and all there ever will be to know and understand."

Imagination is one of the best gifts we have, so why not use it to create, and expand our subconscious with the possibility, that there is more to the world than we can see through our eyes. Energy can be seen and felt. Our inventors have achieved great things out of their imagination or their visualization.

Visualization induces relaxation. Relaxing our mind helps us understand and learn how everything works in our world and beyond the scope of the material world. Without using visualization, we cannot open our minds to symbolism and the concept of how energy works.

Our subconscious is extremely powerful. It brings in the concept of the spirit world and the divine connection of feminine energy. Our subconscious is where our awareness, intuition, emotions, creativity, long-term memory, present mind, and the capability to understand and process the power of our visualization. Using our senses of visualization and our imagination opens up the understanding and the powerful concept of energy. Everything consists of energy, and energy is everywhere.

You must discipline your mind to be observant and aware of everything in your surroundings. Disciplining your mind can be done through meditation. Meditation ensures your mind is relaxed and focused. Listening to your inner self opens the door to your inner stillness and your third eye. Infinite possibilities open by focusing our minds on our inner stillness and the ability to see the energy and use energy.

Our ego is our teacher. If we do not listen to our ego, we cannot let go of what does not serve us. You are ignoring the ability to process the feeling of cognitive dissonance of anger, resentment, jealousy, envy, depression, and victim mentality. Without processing these emotions, you cannot question why these feelings came to the surface. By reflecting on your negative emotions, you realize what steps you need to take, to help you become a better person. You need to stop resisting and learn to let go of the things you cannot control or change.

The feeling of energy comes in all sorts of forms.

Your sense of feeling energy happens when you have sudden shifts in your body temperature.

You feel hot and cold flashes in the body or atmosphere.

You feel pins and needles or tingling in your body.

You feel slight pressure or a tickling sensation.

You feel physical vibrations or the vibrational energy in objects or other people.

Energy Healers use their hands to heal people through vibrational energies in both participants.

Some people can visualize the vibration frequency in people's auras. Most of these sensations are a sense of knowing, and being able to see with and using their third eye.

Signs of Experiencing Energy

Someone experiences energy when seeing colours of light, orbs of light within the peripheral vision in our reality.

Someone experiences energy with the feeling of a vibration or tingling sensation from head to toe.

Experiencing energy is sensing unexplainable warmth or cold hands or feet.

Flashes of light or swirling orbs in the sky are signs of energy in the atmosphere.

Seeing visions, having hallucinations, or geometric shapes and colours with your third eye is a form of experiencing energy.

Seeing an aura or afterimages amongst people or objects is a form of experiencing energy.

Experiencing energy comes in the form of shivers or twitching.

Sudden emotions of the release of tears of joy, crying for no reason, and outbursts of happiness are experiencing energy.

Energy Fields

At the end of a star's life cycle, the star bursts into stardust and cosmic debris in the energy field. The inner core of the star composition is of atoms. When a star explodes, it explodes into various sizes of rock and debris. The chunks of the exploding stars will create additional planets in our solar system. The stardust and chunks are the energy of atoms from the inner core of the exploding star. Studies by Scientists have linked the energy force back to the human body.

Below is a quote from Neil De Grasse Tyson.

"The atoms of our bodies are traceable to the stars that manufactured them in their cores and exploded these enriched ingredients across our galaxy billions of years ago. For this reason, we are biologically connected to every other living thing in the world. We are chemically connected to all molecules on earth. And we are atomically connected to all atoms in the universe. We are not figuratively, and stardust."

Ancient cultures embraced the belief that our body's energy was the essence of our life. The atom is the smallest particle in the universe, and its makeup is ninety-five percent space. Your physical body only represents five percent of who you are. The other ninety-five percent is your vibrational energy. Your vibrational energy is composed of carbon, nitrogen, and oxygen. Many Scientists believe that gases are the substances in every person living here on earth.

Our Body

Our bodies contain all kinds of different types of energy. Our body alone has millions, if not trillions of cells and hormones which make up our organs. Many believe you can channel all this energy in many ways to maintain your body. You can channel this energy through meditation for seeking spiritual awareness, Reiki for healing purposes, and the development of your psychic abilities.

Our biology determines how we process this energy within our body. This energy gives us intellect, and feelings throughout the body, including all our emotions.

Many in the scientific field believe this energy is our life force. It flows through our body into energy centers known as our chakras. These electrical pulses also flow through our meridians and our spinal column. This transformational field is susceptible to all kinds of different energy forces. It holds centuries of timeless energy of essence within our intelligence.

The energy of your Ego takes over the emotional part of you. The Ego inflates or deflates your self-importance. Some people have inflated Egos, which makes them think they are infallible and can do no wrong. The Ego of others shatters their self-confidence and their self-worth. The Ego can and will affect your Spiritual outlook.

You came from a spark of light from the universe to experience life here on earth. In other words, you are an eternal soul that keeps reincarnating here to fulfill your curiosity and enlightenment of yourself Spiritually.

You can go deep within yourself to find the answers to your questions. How many times have you gone to bed with a question? When you woke up in the morning, you have the answer to that question, and you do not know how you could have come up with that answer. The answer to your question was deep inside you because you are the eternal soul of the universe.

Your body picks up the electrical signals and stores that energy.

That information is then filtered to every cell of our body to maintain it physically and psychologically. The Chakra and Meridian systems are excellent examples of the electrical system within our body.

Ways to Understand Energy

1. Be open-minded. Listen to your intuition. Step out of your comfort zone.
2. Belief in possibilities. Believe in yourself. Your power is in your intentions.
3. Visualization. Use your imagination to bring awareness and enlightenment to your life. Meditate.
4. Be an observer. Pay close attention to everything.

The smallest details can mean something. Always be consciously aware of your surroundings.

Medical Fields

Other places you see the use of energy is in the medical profession. Doctors and Technicians use energy to detect and treat diseases. MRIs, EMGs, EEGs, and Cat-scans measure the frequencies of the body's energy, and movements to gain information on a person's health and well-being.

Spirits, Orbs and Angelic Orbs

Energy is all around us. We can see and feel this energy.

Energy fields contain electromagnetic energy that has a higher vibrational frequency.

This higher vibrational frequency is the spirit of people who have passed on. The essence of Angelic energy is in the higher vibrational frequency. This energy can appear to humans as energy orbs or rays of a shaft of light. Humans can feel this energy in their presence. This energy can be unsettling to humans because they fear what they cannot see. These energy forms have no restriction on the physical realm, and the speed they travel at is undetectable to humans.

The most common way a person can see an orb is from the corner of their eye. Little shiny bright white specs of light can flash before your eyes. Angels can travel to this earthly realm through a bright shaft of colourful lights or little orbs.

These orbs can be the spirits of someone you know who has passed on. Your loved ones came to visit you.

The Orbs can be angels, archangels, and spirit guides. They are always near to lend you a hand and watch over you. You have to invite these spirits into your life to help you when you need help. They will not intervene unless you ask them for help. If you do not require assistance, you should always acknowledge them. All you have to do is thank them for their presence.

One Little Prayer I Use:

Thank you, Angels, for reminding me of your presence. I am grateful for your guidance in everything I do, and for ensuring that it is for my highest good and the highest good for all.

Orbs and Rainbows in Photographs

Sometimes the orbs of light can be seen in photographs you took on special occasions. Spheres of light in digital photos can appear in photos taken at any time of day or night. Orbs and rainbows seen on film or Polaroid pictures after development were considered defective and thrown away. These little balls of light can show up later. Orbs were not there before. When you show the pictures to someone, you see the little sphere of lights or an abstract misty shape, or maybe you see a hazy shape in the form of a body in the photo. You think you imagined these things. The funniest thing you know is that there was nothing wrong with the picture.

Many people would say there is something wrong with the photo. Others would wonder who the spirit is. Why would they come to have their photo taken with their family or co-workers?

Energy Shifts and The Awakened State

Our world and humanity have been going through an energy shift for some time, what most Scientists call the Awakening State. Most of the population was unaware of the subtle changes in our thinking and physical well-being. This energy shift is very subtle. The energy shift will happen when there is a physical change in the ethereal world.

Quantum Physics has proven that our body and soul consist of pure energy. Energy is all around us. Everything, including all living creatures and inanimate objects, consist of energy. Most people do not stop to think about how our bodies came to be. They know that it is the natural process of evolution of how we were born into this world. Some people are unaware that our body consists of energy. Everyone and everything have a vibrational frequency. We are unaware our intuition guides us through an energy shift.

We need to be more observant of these subtle energy shifts. Scientists and highly intuitive people believe these energy shifts are happening to prepare us for the new world. Being more observant of our emotions to detect these subtle energy shifts. When you can tell the difference between your emotions, and the collective consciousness, you will start to notice and observe your feelings of emotions as you are processing them internally. Your feelings and awareness will become more noticeable and intense over time.

We are all connected to the universe as one. What ripples out to the universe can be felt in the collective stream, and felt by all who are energetically and consciously aware. Our intentions go out into the universe, and they will return at some point in our lifetime. Being kind to others and showing compassion are positive character traits. The abundance of kindness you show others will flow back to you. Those who live a negative life, and behave negatively toward others, will have the negativity of their unkind deeds returned to them at a more intense level.

In remembrance of 9 11, the terrorist attacks on the Trade Center and other places, Hurricane Katrina, and now the war in Ukraine, flooding, forest fires, and earthquakes are happening in all areas of the world. Empathy creates a collective stream. All our emotions and empathy go into this collective stream of compassion. Compassion felt by everyone collectively happens when we stand together, goodwill will come from these disasters. Many people will do a lot of fundraising, clothing and food drives to help the less fortunate.

When people move into an Awakening State, they will notice many different aspects of their life, and their awareness gradually shifts. People will sense something different about them because they will have started to act and think differently in their everyday life.

There are many things to be aware of when energy shifts happen for a reason.

Listed below are some ways you can recognize energy shifts within you, and others are:

1. When people go through or seek a Kundalini awakening. People experience a dramatic change in their thinking and behaviour. You do not need to be a Buddhist Monk to practice Kundalini.
2. Solar Flares or geomagnetic storms bring energy shifts that would be noticeable through our emotions or physical appearances on earth. A good example would be frightened of tornadoes and storms.
3. Astrological Movements: Eclipses, a full moon, new moons, comets, meteor showers, retrogrades, and astrological events

enhance our intuition and emotions. This often happens without us aware of it.

4. Global Events, Terrorist Attacks, Bombings, and Wars all affect our comprehension and awareness of catastrophic events. These types of events have an impact on our emotions.

5. Natural Disasters: Tornadoes, Hurricanes, and Typhoons are other catastrophic energy shifts that will weigh heavily on our emotions. They pull at our heartstrings with compassion for the less fortunate.

6. Personal Shifts in consciousness can come subtly through our dreams and spiritual awakening through meditation.

7. Personal Life-changes: A move, divorce, death, breakup, having a new baby, illness, a change of job, or an identity change can enhance energy shifts in your immediate life.

8. Adjustments to the Higher Vibrational Frequencies of Energy can create energy shifts in our meditation routine. This energy shift impacts our physical and emotional health.

9. Anyone in a personal transformation will feel energy shifts in their body.

Spiritual awareness and vibrations will be felt throughout the body when the person is awakening.

Signs of Energy Shifts:

1. **Shifts in People:** New people are coming into your life. People from your past are returning.
2. **Shift in Perspective:** When you are inspired to do new things, which will push you out of your comfort zone.
3. **Physiological Shifts in the Body:** Diet changes, cravings, illness, unexpected changes like sudden flu-like symptoms, headaches in the area of the pineal gland, ocular migraines, and blurry vision are all signs commonly felt when an energy shift is taking place within you.
4. **Anxiety:** Anxiety coming out of the blue for no apparent reason is an energy shift.
5. **Shadow Work:** Sudden fears or phobias, old fears returning, and you have no idea why they resurfaced is an energy shift.
6. **Hallucinations or Visions:** Seeing things that are not there are signs of an energy shift. A shift in consciousness will cause visions. These visions have meant something to both the spirit and the person having these visions. Pay close attention to your premonitions and your feelings. These foreboding signs are signs of an enhancement of your intuition or psychic abilities evolving.
7. **Seeing or Feeling Energy:** Seeing orbs, sparks of light, flashes of light, geometrics shapes in the field of vision, colours of light, flashes of colour, vibrating from head to toe, palms gathering energy, seeing a pixelated view of reality, are all symptoms of energy shifts.
8. **Time Shifts:** Time moving ridiculously slow. Time disappears without noticing. Time flying by so quickly is an energy shift. Everyone has had time disappear without us being aware of it.
9. **Vertigo:** Having the feeling the walls or objects are moving in towards you. The feeling of being closed in is an energy

shift. Are dimensions moving or shifting through this energy shift? Are we seeing another dimension?

10. **Something Big is Going to Happen:** The feeling that something big is going to happen, like impending danger. This emotion of fear or excitement may imply your energy is shifting within you.

11. **Moodiness:** Unexpected mood swings without reason. The feeling of anger, sadness, and upset without knowing why is an energy shift.

12. **Hypersensitivity:** Becoming extremely sensitive to light, sound, people, and feeling different frequencies. When your senses become very sharp, it also indicates you are going through an energy shift.

13. **Excess of Change in Energy:** The feeling of you having depleted energy which happens suddenly, or you feel increased energy and think you can do anything, or go on indefinitely, is a definite sign of an energy shift.

14. **Heart Center Shifting:** A feeling of pressure or tightness in the chest, heart palpitations in and around the heart area. This feeling will come and go. It is a sign of an energy shift. **If you have concerns, definitely seek medical help.**

15. **Brain Fog and Spaciness:** The feeling of brain fog, that fuzzy feeling. The feeling of having your head in the clouds and being very much in your thoughts. You do not feel grounded, and your emotions are all over the place. These are signs of energy shifts. Do some meditation to ground and center yourself.

16. **Emotional Purging:** Crying without reason. Purge what does not serve you any longer by doing the following, Spiritual, Mental, Physical, and Emotional Detox. Let go of old emotions. Embrace your feelings. Leave the past in the past. Live in the present. You can embrace the shift.

17. **Mental Clarity:** You have a sudden epiphany of how to solve a problem and you have the answer that came from

nowhere. Universal Self-realization and a light bulb suddenly lights up in your mind, and you can see your future path more clearly.

These signs are all similar to Kundalini Awakening, and they tend to go hand in hand on your way to a spiritual awakening, which can present differently from person to person. The soul's transformation is about recreating yourself. You can use manifestation to create the new you. Kundalini Awakening and all these energy shifts interconnect in many ways, which may not seem obvious in a transitional period. These changes in the ethereal realm make changes in the material world. Pay attention to the subtle change and the patterns. The clarity will be known to you when the time is right, and it will help you understand the transitional period.

Energy Exercises

Exercise One

Rub your hands together for about thirty seconds. Can you feel the warm friction that has built up? Slowly pull your hands away from each other. Do you feel tingling? Is there a static charge? When you touch something like carpet or metal. Do you get a shock? Touch your hair, and slowly pull your hands away. Does your hair try to cling or stand straight up? Keep practicing this technique. The more you do it, the better you will get at creating energy.

Use this technique on yourself to try to heal your aches and pains. Gain permission from people before using this technique on them for healing. Maybe you are an energy healer without you knowing.

Exercise Two

Rub your hands together until you have built up a fair bit of heat, then place your hands on the area you feel pain. Concentrate, meditate, and focus on the healing energy within your hands. After you have built up enough heat between your hands, lay your hands on the area where you have pain. Does the pain feel better? Is the pain gone? Keep practicing. You have to believe in this method for it to work. Many healers use this method. It is all about redirecting energy to where it is needed.

The same principle applies when you are working with the chakras. You manifest the surge of energy, and direct the vibrational energy throughout your chakra system to balance yourself. Get yourself a partner who is willing to practice with you. Staying consciously aware and focusing on what you are trying to manifest is the trick to making this energy work for you.

Exercise Three

Making energy orbs is done the same way, as rubbing your palms together to create energy. This time you slowly pull your hands apart about two inches. Imagine that there is a ball of light between your palms. Use your imagination to make these balls of light smaller or bigger. These energy balls or orbs are called Chi balls. It is a relaxing technique to play around with your energy. You can use this ball of light for healing, the energy in your hands was created by friction.

The energy may bring a sense of calmness and peace. You may have an emotional release. Apply the energy orb to the area that needs healing.

This energy friction is used by healers when they use their hands to heal others. Healers are in tune with the vibrational frequency and the auras of their clients.

Exercise Four

Use your breath to bring you healing qualities. Concentrate on your breathing. Feel the sense of calm come over you as you start to relax. Keep breathing naturally. Concentrate on your heart chakra. Feel the glowing warmth in the center of your chest. Have the energy in your heart chakra flow into your arms, and have the energy flow back into your heart. Continue to focus on your heart chakra, and move the energy down your spine into your solar plexus chakra. Then have the energy flow into your sacral chakra in your abdomen. Now have the energy travel through your spine into your root chakra. Now start the process of moving the energy up into each chakra. Remember to stop along the way to any part of your body you feel you may have a blockage, and apply that healing touch to heal yourself where needed. People have used this healing practice from the beginning of time.

Some people and practitioners swear this method has worked wonders and created miracles for them and in others.

Caution: Make sure you follow your Doctor's advice.

Chapter Four

Auras

What are Auras?

Auras are the composition of energy fields that surround everyone's body. This electromagnetic energy emits from all living things, including people, plant life, and inanimate objects.

People and their auras and everything in this world can take on any of these shapes: a cone shape, egg shape, cocoon shape, oval shape or hallo energy surrounding every person's body.

It is a type of electromagnetic atmosphere. This energy field cannot be seen or felt by most people. A small percentage of humans can feel or see an Aura. People suppress the notion that little puffs of coloured clouds emit and surround their bodies as part of their physical and spiritual essences. This subtle matter of haze that surrounds all living things and objects is the energy that connects us to the universe. This ever-changing energy will never stop cocooning our bodies until the day we die.

In 1939, Russian Scientists Semyon and Valentina Kirlian discovered that cameras could capture people's auras on film.

This method of capturing an auric field on film is known as Kirlian Photography. Some people in the scientific research field discounted this as a scientific discovery, because photographs can be altered or manipulated by outside forces.

Some Scientists proved without a shadow of a doubt that hazy coloured bands surrounded everything. To see these bands of colour, people had to have their pictures taken in a dark place.

Catching the Auras of people turned out to be a significant scientific find on camera. Many Scientists authenticated that auras or the coloured bands in the picture were real.

Now in the digital age, it is harder to manipulate images, and the scientific findings are being accepted and acknowledged as possible.

This vibrational frequency of energy will never leave us. It will stay with us until the day we die.

The vibrational energy frequency of our aura will affect the colours of our colour bands. We can change the colour of our aura bands by the thoughts we create in our minds. Our physical condition will determine the colour of our aura bands also.

A fading or dull aura can indicate sickness, illness, diseases and a dysfunctional manifestation in the auric field before the physical body. It does not mean an impending death or a person having a disease. Fading or a dull aura can also mean a person has an unhealthy or suppressed mind. The person's mind can be full of negativity.

This negativity will keep your aura's vibrational frequency and colour diffused.

Seeing vibrant auras and bands of multiple colours signifies a healthy mind with positive thoughts and a healthy body. A healthy mind and body can enhance a person's way of life.

This energy is considered the subtle body and is the essence of your spirit or soul. The light of your soul emanates from within. Some people can see or feel this energy.

Examining the aura or energy field has revealed different shapes, sizes and various colours. This electromagnetic energy field can be visually seen and felt by some people. They can see and feel or sense the auras of other living things, plants, animals, other peoples' auras and their auras with practice.

These people who can see and sense auras are special people with the six senses of clairvoyance and clairsentient. Clairvoyants are people who can see things that most people cannot. Clairsentience is the ability to sense and feel other people's emotions and auras. Clairvoyance and Clairsentience are a form of psychic abilities that some people have.

Some scientists believe an aura can have an energy field which extends at least seven feet from a person's body. Some of these layers are also known as bodies or planes. This energy field is electromagnetic with vibrational frequencies.

There are several bands of colour in an aura. The bands closest to the body have the most vibrancy. The bands further from the body have a more diffused colour, which is still there for protection around the body. This phenomenon is responsible for the vibrational frequencies of people unable to see or feel their Auras. There is an exception, people like clairvoyants and clairsentient can see, sense and feel other people's Auras.

The Seven Planes of the Aura

Physical Aura Plane

The physical aura plane is the layer that represents our physical health. This aura plane is the band that is closest to our skin. Another name for this plane is the etheric body (layer) or plane. The physical aura is the first plane of your essence. This aura layer it's about one-half inch to two inches, outlining the physical body. The Physical Aura is associated with the First Chakra, The Root Chakra, organs, glands, and meridians of the physical body. The physical plane of your aura also corresponds with the sensations of the physical body. This plane is responsible for the awareness felt around the body, your physical comfort, the pleasure of all kinds and the sensitivity of well-being.

Emotional Aura Plane

This Emotional Plane is also known as the Emotional Body (layer). This plane is all about your emotions. The Emotional Plane is the second plane of your aura and about two to four inches from the physical body. The shape of this aura is oval. The Emotional Layer of your Aura is associated with the Second Chakra, the Sacral Chakra. This emotional plane will change its appearance in colour through a person's emotions. Our feelings and emotions frequently change throughout the day, and the Emotional Layer changes its colour to reflect our moods. If a person is unhappy, the Emotional Body or Plane will appear to have a mark on its surface. If a person is depressed, the Emotional Plane will appear darker than usual. This Aura stores unsettled emotions such as fears, resentment and loneliness.

The second and first layers are in constant communication. When the first layer receives signals from the second layer that it is having emotional issues, the physical body will respond with physical ailments or by reacting with tension, muscle cramps, upset stomach and physical pain. This Emotional Plane is also known as the Vital Level or Layer. The Vital Plane is associated with a rational mind and the ability to understand a situation in a clear and logical linear way.

Mental Aura Plane

The Mental Aura Plane or Body is where the reasoning, logic and thought process forms and takes place. The Mental Plane is the third Aura Layer away from the body.

This Aura band is about four to eight inches from the physical body, and it's associated with the Third Chakra, the Solar Plexus Chakra. Our consciousness, ideas, logic processing, belief systems, and intellect are all processed in this Mental body. Everything is rationalized and validated by mental health when mental issues arise. This plane is also known as the ethereal level. The Mental Plane embraces feelings dealing with emotions such as respect, self-acceptance and self-love.

Astral Aura Plane

The Astral Plane is the fourth body plane, and it is associated with the Fourth Chakra, the Heart Chakra. This fourth layer band is moving outwards away from the body. The Astral Plane is eight to twelve inches from the physical body, and it embraces our spiritual health and stores our capacity to love. The Astral Plane is responsible for our well-being and expansions in our daily life and our life balance.

This Astral bridge is the window into our spirituality. The Astral Plane separates the first three inner layers and the three outer bands of the aura. The Astral Plane is where one's spiritual level, the Divine Mind and One's Serenity resides. One is said to be connected with the divine mind and is enabled to understand the greater universal pattern of the divinity of spirituality.

Etheric Aura Plane

The Etheric Aura Plane is the fifth layer or band away from the body associated with the Fifth Chakra, the Throat Chakra. It is about one to two feet away from the physical body.

This Etheric Body is responsible for sound, vibration, communication and creativity abilities. The Aura Layer acts as a carbon copy of the physical body on the spiritual plane.

This Etheric Plane is how you tap into other people's energies. You use this plane to connect with other like-minded people who are on similar wavelengths as you. The Etheric Plane is the plane that contains your psychic abilities and is your fifth Aura Band or Plane. This plane is associated with the Astral level, and you have loving relationships with others, friends and family.

Celestial Aura Plane

The Celestial body is the sixth plane or band, and it is associated with the Six Chakra, the Third Eye Chakra. This part of your aura band extends two to three feet away from the physical body. The Celestial Plane reflects our subconscious mind. When one embraces meditation and devotional practices, the Physical Mind connects with the Spiritual Mind. Your dreams, enlightenment, and intuition are influenced and stored by the Sixth Plane. People with strong Celestial Auras are very creative.

This Celestial body is where the connection of your memories, dreams, spiritual awareness, intuitive knowledge, trust, honesty, and unconditional love form and are stored. The Celestial body is our connection to something greater than ourselves.

The Celestial Plane is also known as the Lower Mental Level Plane and is associated with the alignment of the divine, which enables you to make commitments to speak, and for one to follow the truth.

Causal Aura Plane or the Ketheric Template

The Causal Aura Plane is the seventh aura band or layer. It is also called the Ketheric Template. The Seventh Chakra, the Crown is associated with the Causal Aura Plane, and it is the last in the aura field. It is where all the other layers harmonize to guide you on your life path. The Causal Plane is where all knowledge and possibilities are possible. It protects and holds all the layers together. The Causal layer is the blueprint of a person's spiritual path. The Ketheric Template reflects all of one's soul's experiences throughout the beginning of time.

The Ketheric Template is our connection to "God, The Creator, or Source" and all that is within each person. The Causal body is about three to five feet away from the physical body. Our conscious and spiritual state determines the distance the Causal Plane is from the body.

This Causal Plane is also known as the Higher Mental Level. This Ketheric Template is associated with Divine Love and Spiritual Ecstasy.

Seeing Auras

It will take time and practice for a person to see theirs and other peoples' Auras. The lighting, or lack of lighting, and a light-coloured background on the wall are preferable to provide the right conditions for seeing Auras.

Sometimes seeing an Aura can take you by surprise.

I remember walking by the bathroom a couple of times one night when the only light in the house that was on was the night light. I unexpectedly saw my reflection in the mirror as I passed the room. I shook my head. I went back to the bathroom and stood in front of the mirror. I could not believe what I saw in the mirror. I saw a brilliant blue light surrounding my reflection in the mirror. At first, I thought I was seeing something that should not be there. I stepped away from the mirror, then I stepped back in front of the mirror, and the brilliant blue light was still there.

I passed the bathroom mirror as I walked down the hall, and I saw my Aura in the mirror once again. My Aura was still a brilliant blue light. When I walked back in front of the mirror again, I did not see my Aura. It did not matter how many times I tried to bring it back that night. I could not.

It will take a lot of determination and practice on your part for you to see your Aura. Don't give up. Keep trying.

Some people can feel auras. They may not see them, but they can sense and feel them. These people are called Clairsentients.

Clairsentients and Clairvoyants can see, sense, and feel other people's Auras.

A Clairvoyant can see the Aura of other people.

Clairsentients can feel or sense your aura's vibrational frequency.

Auras have a very intense vibrational frequency known as Prana, Chi, and your Vital Life Force.

The Vital Life Force links our body to our mind, body and spirit. The Vital Life Force continuously monitors our body for our mental, spiritual and physical health keeping them at the optimal vibrational frequency. If your Aura's vibrational frequency is out of balance, this will bring illness, negative thoughts and disease. Your Aura will become spotty with dark blemishes on the surface, and the aura bands will become murky in colour.

Many people maintain a meditation schedule to balance their Chakras. When you keep your Chakras balanced, your Vital Life Force is in check and retains a higher vibrational frequency.

These special people can feel the vibrational energy surrounding the body, animals, plant life and objects.

Many people use this psychic ability as Reiki Practitioners.

Some people become Clairsentient or Clairvoyant Mediums, or they can do both.

There are many ways you can practice seeing your Aura. You can try these steps or search the Internet for methods.

Method One

1. Find a light-coloured wall, preferably white.
2. Sit quietly with the light behind you, creating a shadow.

3. Take off your eyeglasses. The lenses of your eyeglasses may interfere with seeing the aura outline.

4. Softly gaze at your reflection in the mirror, and widen your peripheral vision while concentrating on a focal point.

5. Use your peripheral vision and look to the outer rim of your shadow without moving your head or body.

6. Make sure your gaze is getting out of focus. Try doing this without blinking.

7. Soon, you should see a fuzzy colour of your outline. Usually, you may have a fuzzy thin white outline.

8. Keep practicing. It may take a little time. Make sure you are relaxed when doing this exercise.

Method Two

1. Lay your hand on a blank white paper.
2. You spread your fingers wide.
3. Then focus on your hand to distort the image of your hand.
4. Look at the space between your fingers without moving or blinking.

Soon you should see the colour of your Aura.

Sometimes it may take a while. With practice, you will get better at it.

Doing exercises for seeing your Aura will strengthen your clairvoyance and clairsentient abilities. These exercises will help with opening up your third eye.

When you see someone else's Aura, it may happen spontaneously. It can happen when you are sitting quietly with friends and co-workers. When you look at a person, you see the subtle band of colour around that person. You could be all alone reading a book then you see a faint colour around your hand or fingers.

You could be with another person when you are reading, or watching television then you see flashes of colour out of the corner of your eye. You have accessed a thing called para-vision. You rub your eyes and blink rapidly, and you take another look to see if you have seen something that is not there.

The second look will rarely confirm what you have seen out of the corner of your eye. The little flashes of light can be someone's Aura, or it may have been orbs of spirits who came to visit you. It is not your imagination. It was your para-vision of orbs and auras.

The fuzzy matter of haze which surrounds your body is there to protect you from harm. Your subconscious knows when something or someone is a threat to you. Those tiny little hairs on your body stand up, and you get goosebumps all over. These are warning signs of impending danger. You should pay closer attention to your surroundings.

Practicing to see your Aura is a great way to develop any of your psychic abilities. You must stay aware, pay attention, stay active, and start your day off right.

The first thing to do in the morning is to acknowledge and count your blessings. Express your gratitude in a morning prayer or a little meditation.

Stay active to keep your senses sharp and your chakras open. Look for ways to help others, play and listen to music often, take a walk outdoors, or walk in nature.

Journal your thoughts, inspirations and feelings. Look for ways to improve your happiness. Look back often to see your progress. All this will help raise your Spiritual Vibration.

The Colour Bands of An Aura

Colours of an Aura

The colours of an Aura correspond with the colours of the seven Chakras.

Some people have described an Aura as being very similar to a rainbow, with its vibrant colours blending into the next colour.

Red

The first layer of your Aura is the colour red. The first layer of your Aura is associated with the First Chakra and the Root Chakra. The Root Chakra is at the base of the spinal column. It has the foundation of influencing your home, career, manifesting powers, sexual energy and values.

Red shades are associated with your physical energy, passion, determination, change, power, survival, courage and action. People with red auras like to take charge of their lives and their understanding of physical realities. They love to be the master of manifesting their desires. They are unafraid to embrace their daring and adventurous side.

People with red Auras will live life to the fullest without regret, for their passion and courage drives them to follow their indulgences. They are not afraid of mortality, and they do not deny themselves the many pleasures that life has to offer.

A person with a red aura is kind-hearted and compassionate for others. Red Auras donates you are working from a stable base, full of energy, and you are good at covering up your emotions.

Dark Red Auras mean you are manifesting negative feelings and energy. You have to let go of the past. Release anything which does not serve you any longer and that you have outgrown.

A darker shade of red may indicate that frustration, anger, or trauma is influencing your life and causing negative thoughts. A person with darker shades of red can tend to be a bully and impulsive. A person may be overworked, have a low vibrational frequency, and show signs of exhaustion.

A flashing red aura means the person is flirtatious and has an inappropriate passionate nature.

Orange Aura

The second layer of your Aura is the colour orange. The second layer of your Aura is associated with the Second Chakra and is in your lower abdomen. This Chakra is the beginning layer of energy of the emotional plane or body. An orange aura and Sacral Chakra are where your creativity and sexual energy are stored.

Orange Aura people can reach out to others through relationships and friendships. People with an orange aura are independent and are a realist.

The orange colours of an Aura represent the center for relationships, friendships and interactions with other people. These people do not take relationships lightly. They value all relationships, whether their relationship is professional or personal.

Orange Aura people value the exchange of money, time, energy, resources and love in their highest regard.

Orange Aura people are very good at teamwork. They are happy and reliable people with a keen sense of perception. Orange Aura people have a dynamic personality that makes it easy to relate to them. They will embrace change with optimism and curiosity.

Orange Aura people will not stay strangers for long. They will make long-lasting friendships quite easily.

Orange aura people are unable to sit stagnated for long. They prefer to be on the move with challenging experiences.

People with orange auras crave newness, freshness and excitement in relationships. They like to keep things fresh and exciting.

When an Aura is a vibrant orange, it indicates the person's ability to integrate into any aspect of their life. It also means the person's eagerness to be enthusiastic and open-minded. They have an optimistic outlook on life.

A bright orange aura is a good sign for people who want to plan a family.

A light orange aura indicates that the person has low self-esteem or they have a sense of loss of their true self. They are out of alignment with their true self when trying to be a people pleaser. They are more adaptable to following others' ways of thoughts and opinions. Light orange auras are susceptible to being bullied.

Murky orange auras the people tend to be overly sensitive, possessive, territorial, harsh and obsessive with their self-image. They tend to be egotistic.

Yellow Aura

The third layer of your Aura is yellow and associated with the Third Chakra. A yellow-coloured aura and Third Chakra resonate with the Solar Plexus Chakra. The solar plexus is a few inches above the navel in a person's abdomen.

Your personality, personal power and Identity are stored in your third layer. It is also where your emotions are stored.

This yellow aura layer and Third Chakra defines who you are in the world. You are creative, curious, and optimistic with a sunny cheery disposition.

Yellow-aura people have high self-esteem, intellect, and personal power.

Yellow aura people are born leaders with high energy levels that motivate others to attain positive qualities for themselves, and to seek a purpose for greatness within their life goals, personally and professionally.

Yellow aura people have mental dexterity, intellectual accomplishments, and controversial abilities with restlessness for change and adventure. Yellow aura people have a strong sense of awareness of who they are.

Yellow aura people inspire others to desire and seek happiness and greatness wherever they can. They shine their radiating positive light and influence others. Yellow aura people have the ability and love to analyze complex concepts and break them down into smaller manageable equations to solve the problem. This love is to engage in complex theories to keep their creative juices flowing.

People with yellow auras are coming into their spiritual awakening, inspiration, creativity, joy and sheer happiness. Their warmth and happiness resonate with their positive outlook on life.

Light yellow, or pale-yellow auras represent spiritual and psychic awareness bringing hope, positivity and new ideas to the forefront.

If your Aura is a bright lemon colour, you may have to face a struggle over your relationship. You have a fear of losing control or self-identity.

A lemon-coloured aura means you have a sharp memory and a focused mind with great business senses. They would do great in the Financial World and related concepts.

Yellow aura people would make great Actors and Actresses with fresh air of openness and communication abilities.

Bright yellow Auras with a hint of brown are people with exceptional mathematic skills and a scientific mind.

An aura with a dark streak of yellow indicates a sign of hyperactivity.

Mustard yellow auras point to resentment and jealousy.

Dark yellow with a streak of brown in their Auras indicates having too much to do and bringing on fatigue.

A metallic yellow aura tends to point to dishonesty, a person who likes to gamble and participate in illegal activities.

A sharp tone of yellow Aura points to a sarcastic person with a logical mind.

Cold shades of yellow Aura indicate people are headstrong and lead by their heads rather than their hearts.

Darker shades of yellow Aura indicate the person tends to be overconfident, a perfectionist and puts themselves down with self-criticism, and it drives them to be a driven-egoistic person.

Shiny gold metallic auras donate the person is full of power and is an inspiration to others. They tend to have spiritual beliefs.

Gold auras mean enlightenment and protection from a higher power. A gold aura brings awareness and practice of spiritual wisdom, knowledge, divinity and intuition.

Green

The fourth aura layer and the Fourth Chakra are green in colour. They resonate with the Heart Chakra. People who have green auras are considered to be compassionate, loving, and have the capacity of generosity for forgiveness. They also have great intuition of the divine.

Green-coloured auras resonate with personal growth. Healing and unconditional love are aspects of people with green Auras. Their life force is robust and powerful. Their life force is detectable by people and animals who are near them.

People with green auras are grounded, naturally drawn to nature, and have healing capabilities.

Whenever you are in the presence of a green aura person, you tend to feel calmer with a sense of peace.

Green aura people can divide their time equally between their creative ambitions and family. A father will be devoted to his children despite how busy he gets chasing his goals.

A Green aura person is self-assertive, which gives them a great sense of responsibility and service when people are in need. A green aura is a bridge between the physical and spiritual planes.

Light green auras stand for healing and compassion.

People with green auras are passive and loving, trustworthy individuals who are generous with love, money, and time.

People with green auras do not like drama, and they usually will not participate in it. They prefer not to waste time. Green aura people express themselves from the heart.

Green aura people are committed to the one they love.

An emerald shade of green indicates a person has natural healing abilities. These people would make fantastic doctors and alternative healers.

Green Aura people tend to have natural luck.

A person with a green aura can have an emotional codependency when the shade or tone starts to change colour.

When green shades of Auras start to turn dull and muddy looking, it tends to mean the person has conflicting emotional feelings.

Murky Green Auras can cause energy shifts in a person where they suck the energy from other peoples' essences because of their pessimism. Their constant complaining and negative attitude turn them into energy vampires. Energy vampires drain the energies from other people causing them to feel tired.

Green auras with a hint of yellow indicate that the person will have traits such as possessiveness and unavailability.

Lime green auras simply unhappy and stressful relationships.

Dark green auras mean negativity is starting to seep into their minds. Anger and jealousy are associated with dark green hues.

Remember that old saying, "Beware of the green-eyed monster."

Pink Auras

Pink Auras are rare. Pink Auras have the same vibrational frequencies as green auras. Pink Auras have a connection to the Heart Chakra. People who have pink auras are bubbly and uplifting. They inspire people with the feeling of comfort to all who are in their presence.

People with pink auras face all challenges with grace and smiling faces. They always have kind words and embrace whoever is in need.

They are nurturing and they care for all of earth's creatures.

Pale pink aura people are gentle. Their loving nature radiates from within them with a sense of calm and peace. They are loving, warm, sensitive, and romantic. Pink Aura people sense that all is well with the world.

People with pink auras are similar to red aura people because pink is another hue of the colour red. The only difference is Pink Aura people are a little softer, or have milder emotions.

Baby pink auras symbolize you are not materialistic and probably a romantic. You like to shower your mate with romantic gestures. Baby pink auras are creative, nurturing, with healing qualities and highly intuitive.

Bright pink auras represent you have a balance between the spiritual world and the material world.

Dark pink aura people have a source of negativity and need to remove it from their life.

Magenta Auras

People with magenta auras are a source of originality with a strong will and are optimistic. They have a great sense of humour. Magenta Auras have an energy field with a frequency of a mixture of blue and red colours and vibrations.

People with magenta auras understand the physical world at large.

These people are highly intuitive, and they have enhanced creative capabilities like no other person. They would do well with their high energy frequency in all creative endeavours.

Magenta aura people thrive with originality and innovation. They are exceptional people who want to be the first to solve a problem or to invent something if possible. They do not like to follow in other peoples' shadows. Peer pressure is not something they would succumb to, and they want to be authentic.

Rich magenta auras are common in Spiritual Leaders. Rich magenta people have acquired wisdom through experiences which they will teach to others so all will benefit. Many older people have rich magenta auras, and this colour indicates maturity. Many younger generations can have rich magenta auras also, and this is a sign the younger person is an old soul. People of any age with magenta auras will thrive in the many challenges they may face as they refuse to be defeated.

A Harsh Magenta Aura is a sign found in false Spiritual Leaders, especially those who try to use their powers to dominate people. These Spiritual leaders have inflated egos and think they know all with a sense of superiority over all humankind.

Blue Auras

The fifth layer of an Aura is linked with the Fifth Chakra and is the colour blue. Blue Auras resonate with the throat Chakra.

Communication with the expression of being heard and understood is common in people with blue auras. A person with a Blue Aura is in the center of natural self-expression and speaks the truth.

People with blue Auras are very intuitive and empathetic, and they can sense and pick up others' vibrational emotions from the auras of other people's inner feelings.

People with blue auras have thoughtful insights when buying gifts for others.

They possess inner wisdom and the understanding of knowledge.

People with blue auras can instinctively feel when something is wrong without knowing all the facts. They have a sense of knowing.

Blue aura people desire to achieve mutual trust, responsibility, honesty and clarity in all relationships, whether they are personal or professional nature.

Blue aura people seek, study and teach the knowledge they acquire.

Royal Blue auras in people suggest natural leadership and a sharp sense of justice.

Brighter blue auras indicate altruism and creativity.

Pale blue auras indicate idealists with intense global visions.

Clearer blue auras indicate objectivity, which makes good teachers or gifted public speakers.

Many Blue Aura people have professions of professional healers, authors, musicians, and other people in entertainment.

A dull shade of blue indicates conservatism and rigidity. These people live by a set of self-imposed rules or rules that parents and mentors integrated into them as they were growing up.

Harsh blue auras may indicate the person may be an autocratic individual who is highly opinionated or intolerant of the lifestyles of others and their beliefs.

The lighter tone of blues suggests the individual's personality is calmer and has a peaceful energy which radiates from them. The calmness may influence others with a sense of peace.

Dark blue auras can mean the person is psychic or a clairvoyant.

Turquoise can mean negative energy, and you are magnetic for negative energy.

Indigo, Purple and Violet Auras

The Sixth layer of the Aura and Six Chakra colour is purple and violet. People with purple and violet auras resonate with the Third Eye Chakra. Indigo, Purple and Violet Aura people are highly intuitive and have a keen sense of knowing. They have psychic abilities. These people can predict the future and the past.

Everyone has a third eye. The third eye is not visible on the outside of the physical body. It is inside the center of a person's forehead and in between your eyebrows.

Indigo has the second-highest vibrational frequency. People with an indigo-coloured aura possess intuitive abilities. Sometimes the person does not believe they have psychic abilities or their abilities has not developed.

People with indigo aura are super sensitive to the energy emitted by others. They have the instinct to perceive what is to happen before it happens.

People with indigo auras have lucid dreams and dreams of premonitions. They have a sensitivity to others' energy which makes them empathetic. Empaths are Highly Sensitive People. (HSPs) for short form.

People with indigo auras will listen to their gut feeling rather than operate from a logical perspective.

These people are natural seekers of knowledge. They see the bigger picture of the universe.

Indigo aura people go with the natural flow and rhythm of life.

They can naturally sense what the truth is from illusion.

People with indigo auras are excellent communicators and can understand the cosmos, its enormous beauty and all its mysteries.

People with a bright indigo aura are more aware of the spiritual realm and unspoken intentions.

A bright blue aura can also point to the psychic abilities of clairvoyance and the intuition of knowing as a clairsentient.

A clear indigo shade of blue indicates the person has an active imagination and a fertile mind.

Older and wiser individuals have deeper shades of indigo blue.

Lavender shades of indigo represent an acknowledgment of a higher power within nature. These people can be herbal specialists.

Blurred indigo auras indicate the person is obsessed with illusions and daydreams. A blurred indigo Aura means the person is soaking up negative energies from other people.

A dark shade of indigo represents the person dealing with disillusionment and isolation.

Hazy shades of indigo mean a disconnect from intuition and self-doubt.

Violet Auras

This colour also resonates with the Crown Chakra and is connected to the highest consciousness. People with violet auras are charismatic and dynamic with compelling personalities. They are visionaries with great ideas for humanity.

They need to be in control with leadership and inspire others to greatness. Violet aura people are an inspiration for people to be their best and manifest whatever they desire. They believe their motivation is to urge people to inspire and lead them to prosperity.

They have the gift of intuition they will use this knowledge for a higher purpose.

Violet aura people are empathetic. Violet Auras have the desire to have a connection with others.

People with violet auras reveal who they are, like an open book. What you see is what you get.

With their high vibrational frequency, they can easily connect with invisible forms of life's energy forces and manifest their desires into reality.

A bright shade of violet is a sign of wisdom and vast knowledge of humanity with empathy for the world.

Violet auras are people's main focus in life is to achieve the highest good for all. They do not have the desire for material possessions beyond what they need for reasonable comfort.

A paler shade of a violet aura person signifies a lack of motivation and incentive. The lack of motivation will lessen the desire to better themselves and prevent accomplishing their grand life plan.

The harsh shade of violet auras will implicate the need for perfectionism with unrealistic goals. They will not be able to handle the imperfections of their own and others' daily lives.

Dull violet auras are an indication of depression setting in, and overtaking their thought processes leading to a lack of motivation to accomplish their goals.

White Auras

The Seventh Layer of the Aura and the Seventh Chakra resonate with the white colour. White Auras resonate with the Crown Chakra. The Crown Chakra is located directly above your head. The vibrational frequency of a white aura is All Is One and Oneness for the higher power of God or Source. White auras also symbolize purity.

A few white aura people achieved their highest spiritual self when they freed themselves of all obstacles. They need to defeat all the challenges life has to offer here on earth. They have transcended without limitations into their Spiritual Self for their highest and the highest good for all.

A pure white aura is very rare. Only a hand full of people in the physical realm have reached the highest level of spirituality.

White aura people reach the state of spiritual enlightenment when in tune with the cosmos and all its energies. People who have maintained this spiritual enlightenment have no concern over the materialistic ambitions of the world.

People with white auras are all about purity and honesty. They come from a place of non-judgment, positivity and genuine enlightenment that radiates from within them in everything they do.

White aura people follow a unique spiritual path without any judgment or question. The people with white auras are unique and hold the highest regard and recognition of their spirituality.

Fame will not inflate their sense of self-worth or ego. They will modestly continue with their life as it is.

Misty white auras indicate a person seeking spiritual answers about the universe.

Some white-aura people will also have a mixture of other colours in their Aura.

Black Auras

Black Auras resonate with negative energy, thoughts and emotions. People with black auras may be harbouring ill feelings about something or someone.

People with black auras indicate the energy flow through their chakras may be blocked. The turmoil or chaos in your life must be dealt with and removed.

Detecting Auras in People

You might be able to detect the colour of a person's aura without seeing their aura. You can observe a person and how they interact with people, and by the colour of the clothes they wear. A person who wears blue or green a lot has a peaceful outlook. They tend to go with the flow and take everything in stride. They are slower to anger.

A person who wears reds and blacks a lot is easy to anger. The way they interact with people and the colour of their aura is a tell-a-tale sign that the person may have an illness and should see a doctor. Depression is common when people wear red or black clothing. Anger is another aspect of people wearing red or black clothes. It is interesting how the choice and colour of your clothing can affect your aura and vibrational frequency.

One afternoon, a visitor stopped by to have tea. I looked at my visitor and I could see a beautiful green aura around her. I told her about her green aura, and she was shocked. I explained to her a green Aura was a good thing.

The conditions were perfect to see her aura. Her vibrational frequency was high and it emitted a green aura all around her. This woman is a quiet, peaceful and happy-go-lucky person with a smile for everyone she meets.

All a person needs to do is sit in front of a person or object. Do not look directly at the person or thing. Look at the person, then focus on the area beyond their physical body, the outline of their body. Concentrate and focus. You may be able to see the person's or an object's aura. Notice the hazy or fuzzy colour around your subject.

Keep trying.

Aura colour definitions are in another section of the book, The Colour Bands of Auras.

Dark, murky or dull colours in a person's aura may also be a warning of impending illnesses.

If someone suddenly changes the colours of their wardrobe, this may be a sign that the person may be ill and should see their doctor. These people will have a sudden or gradual shift in their mood, energy and outlook. A person does not have to see a person's aura to know when something is off with that person. It could be as simple as losing their purpose of identity and not standing up for themselves. They may be easy targets for bullies or manipulators.

Spring and summertime bring the promise of new birth. Nature is renewing the vibrant colours and growth of everything that flourishes from the earth. With the promise of spring, our moods change with an uplifting and encouraging outlook. The warmth and brightness accompanied by new growth inspire people with positive energy.

What do you feel when you go outside and look up at the sky? The sky is bright blue with a few clouds.

Your spirit soars with positive feelings and energy, and you feel pretty good about yourself and the universe.

The sky is full of dark heavy clouds. Your inner self does not feel so positive and uplifted. You feel down and out of sorts.

Scientists have a theory the colours in a rainbow are the same as a person's aura, and these colours also resonate with our Chakra System.

The different shades of these vibrant colours can significantly change our mood to positive thoughts and energy. When the colour pales to the point of being non-existent, our emotions will change to the negative side, leading to negative thoughts and depression. Our aura can bring a peaceful feeling to our body and mind or warn us of impending danger.

The essence and well-being of our body are when our aura's colour and vibrational frequency are in sync.

Adding meditation into your daily practice and life is a way to balance your mind, body, and soul. You will be more peaceful and have a sense of well-being. Meditation will raise your vibrations to the highest level of spirituality and your highest good and the highest good for all.

You need to pay attention to your thoughts. Positive thoughts can easily change in a heartbeat. Negative influences in the world and within your life will creep in and try to ruin your day. It could be a person in your life, or you can pick up the negativity from watching the News or TV programs. You must be aware of your thoughts and turn your thought process back to the positive side again. Doing so will keep your mind, body, soul and aura healthy.

Most people have an active life, and you deserve a break once in a while. Busy people have an easier time keeping balance in their life. Active people are more mindful and spiritual. They have a positive and healthy aura, as they spend less time in front of a TV.

Couch potatoes are neither well-balanced nor have healthy Auras. They have too much time on their hands to watch TV. Watching TV insights negative thoughts that creep in and help promote thoughts of negativity.

You can start your day out by making time to meditate.

Make a Gratitude List, listing everything that you are grateful for.

Look for ways you can be a service to others and help them out.

Listen to uplifting music.

Take a nature walk.

Start a journal to record your thoughts. Recording your thoughts will help you find your negative triggers.

Exercises for Seeing Auras

Here you will find some exercises to help you to see your aura.

The first step is to find some alone time. Go to some place quiet without distraction.

Your alone time could be when and where you practice your Meditation. When you meditate, you open yourself to the experiences of quietening the mind. You become aware of those intrusive thoughts and the everyday noise. You have to block out the chatter of your hectic daily life. Everyone has a to-do list and obligations of work which unbalances one's equilibrium. Meditation helps you to be quiet so you can focus on hearing your inner spiritual self and sense the etheric field.

Meditation allows you to ascend to your higher spiritual consciousness of awareness. This awareness will help enable you to tap into your hidden psychic abilities.

Jigam

You can use this technique called Jigam, an ancient Korean method. The word Jigam, when translated into English, it means "to stop thoughts and emotions." You have to stop your thoughts and emotions so you can feel, see and sense this subtle vibrational energy of your aura.

Begin with a brief meditation to make sure you are grounded and centered.

Do this grounding part of the exercise.

Visualize that you are growing roots from the palms of your

hands and feet. Make sure these roots are taking root into the ground, and it is centering you.

Use this meditation exercise to help you practice quietening the mental chatter.

Quieting the Mental Chatter

Jigam Exercises:

Rap Your Fingers:

Take a few deep breaths, in and out, as if you are going into Meditation. Relax your shoulders, wrists, and fingers.

Rap the tips of your fingers gently against each other for about 60 seconds. It will feel like you are trying to wake up your fingers as if they had fallen asleep.

You will feel the energy flowing into your fingers.

You will begin to feel an energetic vibration between your hands. It may feel like pins and needles or a warm sensation.

Try to pull your fingers slightly apart. Do you feel a slight energetic pull as if your fingers are losing contact?

The energy you sense is part of your auric field's vibrational frequency.

Do this exercise often. The more you do this exercise, the easier it will become to detect the energy fields and their vibrational frequency.

Wringing Your Wrists:

Take some deep breaths and exhale a few times to relax your body.

Relax your hands and gently clasp your other wrist with your other hand.

Quickly twist your wrist several times until you feel friction.

Make sure you keep both hands in a relaxed state.

Only use light pressure, so you will not cause a friction burn.

Do this until you feel the energy flowing through both hands.

This exercise will increase your sensitivity. It helps you feel and detect energy fields and their vibrational frequencies.

Rubbing of the Palms:

Take a couple of deep breaths and relax.

Rub both hands vigorously together.

Notice the warmth and tingling sensation with friction between both hands.

Gently pull your hands away from each other slowly and gently.

Notice how they feel.

Slowly put both hands back together and notice how they feel.

The closer your hands get to each other, the more the energy wants to come together as one energy force instead of two.

Some people can manifest an energy ball in between their hands. A Chi Ball.

With this step, you can use visualization to see if you can manifest your energy ball.

The more you practice these techniques, the more you can recognize the different feelings of energy. You can tap into it and awaken your psychic abilities.

Relieving Pain

Try rubbing your palms together for this exercise to relieve pain. When your hands are warm and fully charged, put your hands on the spot where you have pain.

Focus on that same spot, and visualize your hands delivering healing to that area of the body.

Do this exercise repeatedly to relieve pain for yourself and others. Do not practice this exercise on other people without their permission. You do not want to violate other's psyches.

It may not heal the area, but it will help relieve some pain.

If you can do this, one of your psychic gifts could be you are a healer.

Some of these Psychic Healers are in the medical field, as Doctors and Reiki Practitioners.

By doing these exercises often, you can open yourself up too many other psychic abilities.

You have to start small and then work yourself up the psychic ladder. It will take time and patience to achieve this ability.

Use this healing technique to help unblock your Chakra. Your Chakra system has a lot to do with your psychic abilities. Your mental and physical well-being are compromised when you have a blocked Chakra. You are out of balance.

Meditate, exercise and use visualization to bring your Chakra back into balance.

After you balance your Chakra, you can and will develop your senses to your higher awareness and higher self.

These exercises are a great way to recognize the energy you can create yourself.

What about when you walked across a carpet? You immediately received a shock because of the friction you created between the carpeting and your socks. You made that energy.

With Meditation, paying attention to your body, and practicing these simple little exercises, you will develop your psychic abilities.

It is all about you being sensitively aware of your inner self and surroundings.

Cleansing your Aura

Everyone needs to cleanse their Aura whether they know it or not. You pick up vibrations from everyone and everything you come into contact with. All people, animals, and objects carry and emit positive or negative vibrations. The positive vibrations do not cause a problem with your Aura. It is the negative ones that can cause you to worry.

Negativity is everywhere you go. It does not have to be harmful.

It could be as simple as walking into a Department Store. People in the store are having a stressful day and are emitting negative vibes. Maybe, someone at work is having a bad day, and the negative vibes transferred to you. You begin to have a negative day. Your Aura is picking up all this negative energy. You become stressed and unhappy without realizing it. Your positivity and energy start to waver, with this feeling of negativity unbalancing you, and your sense of wellness diminishes. You need to cleanse your Aura and bring back your positive happy outlook back into your life.

There are several methods you can use to cleanse your Aura.

The methods are listed on next page.

Nature

Use nature to cleanse your Aura. A nature walk will help tremendously.

Listen to the birds singing, the wind swaying tree branches and leaves rustling.

The sounds of crickets or frogs croaking are music to your ear.

The lapping of the water against the shoreline or the trickling water in a creek soothes your mind.

These can bring relief from stress, and a sense of balance returning into your life.

Meditation in nature can cleanse your Aura by using positive thoughts.

Swimming in natural water, rivers, lakes, or oceans can cleanse your Aura. The water will wash your Aura clean and remove all the negativity by relaxing you and bringing back a sense of peace and balance into your life.

While you are in the water, try meditating, it will bring you comfort.

Swimming in the salt water of an ocean or pool would be most beneficial. If swimming in salt water is not possible, swimming in natural water will do just fine.

Soak in a bath with Epsom salt or sea salt is an alternate way to cleanse your Aura.

Using essential oils in bath water or the smell of incense is also beneficial.

Dim the light, or using scented, or unscented candles to light the room can be soothing, and beneficial.

Start meditating to bring a sense of well-being and serenity to yourself. Bathing in the salt water and meditating will cleanse your Aura.

You can use incense if you like instead of scented candles.

You can use meditation soundtracks to cleanse your Aura.

Check the Internet for Aura-cleansing videos.

Visualization and Body Scan

You can use visualization to cleanse your Aura.

1. Lie in a quiet room, on a bed or the floor. Whichever is more comfortable for you? The place must be without distraction.
2. Take fifteen minutes. Set a timer if you want to time yourself. Sometimes this may defeat the purpose of quiet time. You may be concentrating on the timer going off instead of meditating.
3. Focus on your breathing. Breathe in through your nose, hold your breath for a few seconds, then exhale through your mouth for a few seconds. Repeat inhaling and exhaling until you feel relaxed. Feel the rise and fall of your chest and stomach.
4. When you are relaxed, continue breathing in and exhaling. Visualize a part of your body one at a time until you reach

your toes. Note how each body part feels when you stop there to concentrate on them. Do a body scan.

5. Now, in your mind, picture a bright light above your forehead.

6. Scan your whole body with this white light. Savour the warmth of the white light as it penetrates each part of your body as the light cleanses your Aura.

7. Sense the peace, warmth, and protection from the white light when it erases all the negative vibes, and emotions you have encountered throughout your day.

Your Aura acts like a magnet, attracting all the positive and negative vibrations in your orbital space. Eventually, you will encounter negative vibrations, and aura cleansing will be needed to bring back peace, and contentment, and to balance your life.

The variation of time limits does not exist in between cleansing an Aura. You can clean your Aura daily when you take a shower or bath. You can set a time for your aura cleansing rituals.

Chapter Five

Black Energy

The world is not immune to Black Energy.

There are many movies out there that depict the dark side of life. You see it through horror movies and the evil or wrong actions of people from a large part of the population. People doing horrendous things to other people every day is getting worse and increasing at an alarming rate.

There are haunted houses, and things will move by themselves. It does not happen just in movies. They do happen in real life. Demonic forces from the subtle planes of existence frighten people every day. These forces create events and situations in our daily lives that seem to be supernatural or paranormal phenomena.

The extraordinary orchestrations of these attacks can be so dramatic, and they leave an impression on a person's psyche.

Psychic attacks left unchecked can cause a person with depression and addictions to go into despair, where they can see no way to improve their life.

The feeling of unworthiness and depression can sometimes lead to suicide or long-term hospitalization. A person affected by dark energy has a dynamic impact on a family by creating disharmony and hardship.

These black energies have left deep-seated discord in people from all walks of life here on the physical plane. This dark energy has created Spiritual impurities in the environment.

What is Black or Dark Energy?

Kali shaki is also known as Black or Dark Energy. (Kali means Black, and Shaki means Energy).

It is a form of Energy that exists on subtle planes and on earth. This Energy attacks people, all living things, and inanimate objects to cause fear and harm. This negative energy is a dark entity's primary weapon of control over others.

A recently deceased person can be attacked or an attacker. In the shock and confusion of the events surrounding their death, their mind may be unable to comprehend what has happened to them, or they are not ready to depart this world.

The Universe has three components called Sattva, Raga and Tama. Creation, visible and invisible.

Sattva creates spirituality and purity in people. Raja enables action, and Tama induces spiritual ignorance and inertia. The subtle vibrations that emanate from everything are either positive or negative energies. Depending on the dominant components that made them, they can be either negative or positive energies.

Tama-predominate is black energy or impure spiritual energy. Raga spreads negative energy through its vibrations.

The source of black or dark energy is a higher level of negative energies, and resides in hell's lower subtle regions. The spirits of this region practice gaining more dark energy for themselves.

Subtle Sorcerers are also known as mantriks. They are the stronger negative energies, that provide energy to ghosts of lower levels to carry out tasks for them. The lower negative ghost please the higher levels of mantriks to gain access to the reservoirs of the higher levels of negative energy.

The Subtle Sorcerers and mantriks acquire an immense amount of unlimited source of black energy. They can use this energy from the lower realms of hell to create wide-scale things like pandemics, the Corona Virus, and natural disasters such as Earthquakes and Tsunamis. They can affect larger scales of the population at the same time with their immense strength of black energy, and that includes war.

Energy is neither good nor bad. Energy can be used for good and righteous intentions, creating Spiritual enlightenment. Spiritual enlightenment is a higher purpose of serving God, a Source, or a Higher Being.

Black Energy is stated as black, dark, and evil. Unrighteous spirits seek out newly departed souls to corrupt and bring them over to their side. These evil spirits will try to use lost wandering souls to fulfill their evil intentions, which they inflict on unsuspecting people. Black Energy will penetrate the minds of ghosts and people to make them do their evil intentions of creating chaos, unrighteousness and misfortune throughout the world.

Signs of Black Energy in People

The signs of being affected by dark energy:

Symptoms of Attacks:

Physically: You feel lethargy, weakness, headaches, unwell feelings, and undiagnosed ailments and diseases are all signs of the effect of dark energy.

Psychological: The feeling of anger, anxiety, or depression, including any mental illness such as addictions or schizophrenia.

Spiritual: The feeling that you do not want anything to do with spiritual practices.

Block in the Pren Shaki (vital energy) in the body causes many obstacles for the person. Demonic possession of a person is possible.

A black covering of energy reduces the clarity of thought and creates heaviness in the head. A black covering of dark energy will emerge inside a person's body through penetrating thoughts. Attacks can happen outside of a person's body.

In a subtle battle of spiritual strength, a spiritual and physical body can succumb to a spiritual attack. Higher levels of negative energies use black energy to Spiritually pollute a person, environment or premises.

Black entities will take advantage of your negative thinking. Black entities will stop at nothing to take control of a person's personality and will cause defeating bouts of anger to blow everything out of proportion.

Types of black energies:

First:

Generic Black Energy: This energy creates illness and violence.

Second:

Illusory (mavin's) Vibrations: This energy distorts negative black energy into positive and beneficial illusions. There is the belief that Cola and makeup carry negative energies. This black energy is more dangerous than generic black energy. This harmful energy can make appealing things appear normal.

Third:

Enticing (morphine) Vibrations:

Black energy can possess a person to make that person alluring and seductive, manifesting excessive seductive sexual thoughts. Enticing energy can propel a person to stardom, which creates mass influence on a large scale of the population in society.

The best way to protect yourself from dark energies is to engage in daily spiritual practice and implement spiritual healing properties.

Maintaining a Spiritual belief will help you fight off an attack from dark energy, and it is your best defense.

Negative Energy

Negative or Dark Energy and Evil Spirits

Do you believe in negative, dark, or evil energies?

I do! I have seen it on several occasions. Some Psychics may have a different opinion, and that is their prerogative.

When I was younger, I did see dark shadows that terrified me. Some dark shadows or puffs of little black clouds appeared in front of me. I told the adults about the incident, but they did not believe me. It could be that they chose not to believe me out of fear.

These dark entities do exist!

The majority of the population in the world does not believe in dark and evil entities. Why do all Psychics believe in self-protection? Some Scientists think meditating to their highest consciousness may leave you unguarded to dark entities. Without Spiritual protection, you are leaving yourself open to attacks.

You have a greater chance of being attacked by dark entities if people mess around with dark magic and spells, by themselves or with occults, and if you play with Ouija boards, you are inviting trouble. You leave yourself open to evil, dark and negative energies. You may open a portal that you may not be able to close. Opening a portal is like leaving your house doors wide open and giving your neighbours or thieves access to your home twenty-four-seven. That is what it would be like if you messed around with those things.

Researchers and Psychic Mediums believe people who search for these dark entities will find them. They risk being attacked or possessed.

I know some people do not believe in possession by an evil spirit. The Catholic Church, Spiritual Scientific Researchers, and I think people can and do get possessed.

Priests and Researchers have documented that they have undergone attacks during exorcisms.

According to a show called Sixty Minutes I watched recently. Priests and Researchers believe possession is on the rise because there are fewer Spiritual people than non-believers. Some non-believers can and do get attacked or possessed by dark entities.

60 Minutes interviewed a few Priests in different locations in the United States. They said in the interview they get up to thirty-five calls a week from people fearing they are possessed or have a dark soul attached to them. Now that is a scary thought.

Negativity can be from a dark spirit or the living. It can weigh you down and cause negative thoughts, depression and health problems. There is a famous saying I have heard from many people, "It is not the dead you have to fear. It is the living." It could be as simple as having negative people in your life. The negativity could come from your parents, siblings, co-workers or friends. Some people believe your Spiritual Ancestral Family or a previous life you may have lived here on earth, all can be the source of the dark, and negative thoughts and attacks.

Negative people in your life are Energy Vampires and feed off the positive and Spiritual Enlightened people. The energy vampires cannot stand anyone to be happy, or the Spiritually enlightened people. The vampires are envious of happiness. The bright light that shines through you and the positivity that exudes from you threaten them. The vampires want to bring you down to their level of unhappiness.

Remember back to a time when you were happy, excited, flowing full of positive energy, and you entered a room where you suddenly felt tired, unwell, or physically drained.

The reason behind this, the room had some energy vampires, and they depleted your white energy from you.

If this has happened to you, you are more than likely an Empath or a Sensitive Soul. If you are, then you understand what I am talking about.

Demonic Possession

Under the influences of a Ghost and Demonic Possession:

Being influenced by Ghosts or Demonic Possession can present itself in many ways. It can affect you spiritually, physically, mentally and intellectually. Possession will make it very difficult for you to concentrate. The ghost merge with your consciousness to control you, and make you do things you usually would not, and things of no spiritual aspect.

Inhabiting the mind is a common trait of Ghosts to prevent Spiritual Practices.

Ghosts, dark energy, negative energy, and demons can stimulate or cloud a person's mind using their black energies for their gain.

These energies can produce a skin rash causing the person to be unwilling to interact with family members and friends. The affected person will not go out publicly or socialize. The Ghosts' objective is to make the affected person very unhappy. It can lead to depression, which leads to withdrawal from normal daily activities.

Attacks of black energies and Ghosts can be deadlier than any poisonous gas manufactured to this day.

The black covering of black energy can be like someone walking into a room full of poisonous gas. Once black energy has covered you, the accuracy and intensity will determine the severity and duration.

With demonic possession, the black energy has merged with the consciousness of the affected person. Demonic possession will physically take over every aspect of that person's free will, and use that person to do unimaginable things for its desired objectives.

A person is possessed either from the outside or from the inside their body. There is no difference in the intensity of the possession. A possessed person from the inside, the demon can control the movements of that person's physical body. That person will remain at the mercy of the demon. The person possessed usually does not know they are possessed. The person will act out of character and be unaware of it.

Subtle Sorcerer

Subtle Sorcerer (Mantriks)

Subtle Sorcerers are the highest ghosts (demons, devils, negative energies etc.).

Their spiritual strength is a hundred thousand and into infinity. Subtle sorcerers are extremely powerful, and their power is almost comparable to that of the manifest form of God.

The spirits of this calibre are working toward supremacy. They want to rule over the subtle etheric regions and all regions of the earth. They are trying to build the order of unrighteousness. The subtle sorcerers work through the lesser ranking of ghosts. They use the weaker slaves to obtain their objective. They have a network of communication through the different levels of all ghost regions.

A lower-ranking ghost has almost no energy strength. What energy it has will deplete very quickly, and it has to restore its power. The entity will get its energy source from the next higher level of dark energy of ghosts.

A subtle sorcerer will come to the rescue to replenish the dark energy of the next lower-ranking ghost, when needed for them to complete its directives from a higher entity.

The subtle sorcerer ghost does not usually possess average humans unless they are on the downward spiral of humanity. It would be almost impossible to recognize if the sorcerer inhabits a person.

People with ninety percent spirituality or the six sense may be able to detect the possession of the person.

Subtle Sorcerers and a lower-ranking ghost will intercede with humans to instigate wars, and genocides and bring on mass destruction through natural disasters. The subtle sorcerers will target Saints and Spiritual Seekers of God who are dedicated to actively spread Spirituality.

By manipulating Absolute Cosmic Principals, subtle sorcerers can create floods, tsunamis, earthquakes, and much more natural destructions, and even cause earth wars.

Possession of humans is unlikely to be from subtle sorcerers, but influencing humans can be done from the outside. Subtle sorcerers can maneuver other levels of ghosts to do the work of possessing a human, and use them for their gain of spreading evil.

When a subtle sorcerer becomes overpowered, they recede to the deepest part of hell to meditate to regain their strength.

The subtle sorcerers reside in one of the seven regions of hell. This region is also known as Patal. They live in the second region of hell, the underworld, where the vibrational frequency matches their frequency. This frequency is known as the Raja-Tama vibration.

A Subtle Sorcerer can assume any form they please to manifest and acquire what they desire. They can take on a physical form as a human or animal. Their exposure to humans depends on their comfort with being seen and interacting with humans. The subtle sorcerer depends on the lower-level ghost to achieve what they want.

The subtle sorcerer's aura radiates their immense spiritual energy and is comparable to a Saint.

Subtle Sorcerers guard their secrets. They are very cunning and highly skilled at scheming. They learn the rituals of others without disclosing their secrets of how they obtained their knowledge. During meditation, they can concentrate on their relevant thoughts to manifest and complete whatever action they desire. Total control over humans is conducive to furthering their objectives.

A subtle sorcerer will sit in meditation for hours. They will generate immense negative spiritual energy through many different postures. The dark energy they acquire can be transmitted in any desired direction to maintain respective postures.

The mantras they use in meditation have a base tone and center the black energy throughout their bodies. They use tantra to harness spiritual power to use for worldly acquisitions. They manifest illusionary forms with the use of meditation. Subtle Sorcerers can influence people through meditation to bring their desire to fruition. They have the intense demoniacal pleasure of disrupting the social structure of evolution.

The Subtle Sorcerers affect humans in many different ways. One way is by causing imbalances in atmospheric temperatures. This imbalance will cause extreme restlessness and make the environment saturated with black energy inducing destructive anti-social behaviour and activities.

The subtle sorcerers love to cause physical distress to humans by infiltrating their minds and altering their thought processes. Placing thoughts of suicide, and there is no place for their existence to thrive.

They can create mutant strains of viruses, as pandemics worldwide.

They bring on the work and infuse unrighteousness in society by possessing key people to implement their directives to create worldwide havoc. The subtle sorcerer affects humanity by creating terrorists, and leaders with international structures and using them like puppets to manufacture weapons of mass destruction, and to use them.

Subtle Sorcerers are extremely difficult to abolish. Saints and people with ninety-five percent spirituality can overpower these menacing dark entities, and then we may have a fighting chance to rid the world of negativity.

The Common Ghost

Common Ghosts (Shut)

The common ghost is the lowest type of ghost in the hierarchy of ghosts. Their strength is about one.

A common ghost has relatively very low strength. About thirty percent of the population can be affected by these types of ghosts or possessed by them. Some of these ghosts can be your departed loved ones or one of your Ancestors, or maybe the ghost has an attachment to the residence.

The common ghost resides in the subtle region where they have the same frequency and vibrations that match their own. Common ghosts will take up residence in dilapidated houses, pubs and places of entertainment, ditches, canals, or residents that resonate with their type of qualities such as habits and desires. The common ghost changes different residents daily to fulfill their desires.

The ghost of a departed loved one can remain earthbound for many years because of unfinished business with a person, family or business partner. Another reason their spirit stays earthbound is the level of spirituality was not high enough to enter Heaven.

Their determination to look after the people they love is a strong motivating factor. Whatever their reasons are not to cross over and stay earthbound depends on the life that person had lived previously.

For some ghosts, their life ended suddenly. Some ghosts remain earthbound to cause havoc in some person's life out of pure meanness. The longer a common ghost stays earthbound, the risk of attacks is greater to higher levels of dark and negative energies. The higher level of dark and negative energies used the common ghost to do their work to corrupt the newly departed and lost souls, who do not recognize they have passed on.

Some Ancestors remain earthbound to cause trouble with descendants. Their reason for staying is fueled by the dark negative energies of ghosts from higher levels ghosts.

Physical Features of a Common Ghost

Common Ghosts can take on any shape and colour depending on their desired result and how they plan to expose themselves. Often their manifesting matches the original body image they had on earth. When common ghosts intend to frighten people, they can take a more amorphous shape. The variations of their regular image are limited to their level of spiritual energy, which is very low. Very sensitive people can see and sense Common Ghosts.

Common Ghosts are often seen near ground level or appear to be floating near ground level.

Mental Features

Common Ghosts tend to stay around ghosts of those with the same vibrations and personality. They tend to flock together.

Most relatives would like to believe that their departed loved ones made their complete journey to Heaven. Common ghosts have restless natures and do not remain in one place very long. They tend to be constantly on the move.

Common Ghosts are very fond of worldly pleasures and desires. When they manifest and possess a person, they seek attention by shouting and making loud noises and sounds. They like to show appreciation by clapping their hands. They love to make disturbances, play pranks and have fun.

Common Ghosts do not usually attack humans. They like to watch the reactions of the living. They constantly love to cause some trouble for the living by frightening them and to fulfill their desires through people.

Common ghosts cannot work on their own. They need the strength provided by the higher-level ghosts for doing the tasks like conveying messages to superior ghosts in various places.

They do not practice spirituality to become more powerful than dark energies. The energy is provided to the common ghost by demons, devils, and negative energies.

A departed Ancestor can be a common ghost with dark energies causing havoc for the living, or they can be a spiritual being visiting.

Nevertheless, they are on the same level regardless of their spiritual strength as in the region they reside.

Affects of Common Ghost

How does a Common Ghost Affect the Living?

1. Possessing a person, using their body to fulfill the dark energies desires for sex, food, alcohol, etc.
2. Materializing in front of the living.
3. Temporarily possessing animals to frighten or attack the living.
4. Changing the subtle pressure in the atmosphere causes it to become cloudy with a black mist. Ghosts cause disturbances in a family, like fighting, rows and family members unable to work together as a family.
5. Common ghosts can spoil food.
6. They move things, making the objects harder to locate.
7. Making objects fall or tip over.
8. They remove things and money from the living by orders from a superior ghost.
9. They can make strange noises by jumping on ceilings and walls.
10. They can generate strange and loud noises through negative frequencies.
11. They can shove the living when they are walking.
12. Make people talk in their sleep.
13. Bed wetting at night.
14. They touch the living causing various sensations, such as giddiness, your little hairs standing up, etc.
15. When a person is undergoing spiritual healing, the possessed person will stomp their feet and clap their hands.
16. White fog appearing in a darkened room temporarily affects the person's memory of what they were doing.
17. Causing sudden personality changes like throwing tantrums, cursing and shouting.
18. A fear of entering a place of worship and worshiping articles.

Things to Use to Help Protect Yourself

Burn Jasmine incenses, sprinkle Holy Water and apply Holy Ash on the head and back of individuals to protect yourself or an affected person.

Sprinkle Holy Water and use common Frankincense Incense for a location and environment.

Some of these afflictions result from a past life brought in at birth to the here and now.

Demons

Demons (Rakish and Amur)

Demons have a strength of ten to one hundred and can affect fifty percent of the world's population. They gain their strength through their spiritual practice to cause harm to humanity.

Demons are second in the hierarchy of ghosts. Some Ancestors may inhabit this category.

Demons prefer to live alone in solitary places, rooftops, attics, factories and caves.

People possessed by demons will exhibit these traits, shuffling gait and stamping legs to get attention. The person may throw objects and make loud sounds with their eyes closed.

1. Demons are very Arrogant. Demons love to be the boss over lower-energy ghosts.
2. Demons are impatient and short-tempered, and they growl if attacked.
3. Demons satisfy their cravings for food through foodstuff obtained by others.
4. Demons are lazy and lethargic.
5. Mantriks, Subtle Sorcerers, take delight in punishing Demons
6. Demons resort to rape to satisfy their lust.
7. Demons are not commonly known to resort to extravagant acts.
8. Demons reluctantly participate in rituals to assimilate black energy from spiritual practice. They will not take up inferior jobs, only when they are ordered to by Subtle-Sorcerers.
9. Demons transmit dark energy with explosive expertise.

10. Demons influence humans intending to cause harm to mankind by transmitting distressing sounds. One of the sounds is imitating earthquakes. Hearing the sound of working machinery when there is no possible way that it can be.

11. When a demon is in your presence, there will be a foul smell, and you will not be able to trace it back to a source.

12. When demons are angry, they can create holes and cracks in walls. When a person meditates and chants, a demon can manifest dampness under that person.

13. Person can be affected by demons, with symptoms like loss of appetite, itchy skin, and giddiness. People have heard constant distressing sounds near a person's ears and some numbness in their ears due to weird sounds.

14. When meditating, a person can feel that an entity is touching and pushing them.

15. Demons can wake people by touching them.

16. There has been sleep loss reported during the night or daytime.

17. Someone may have thoughts of assaulting another person.

18. When a demon affects people, that person will not let others practice spirituality.

If you suspect someone may be affected by a demon, you can blow Holy Ash into their face and onto their back. The use of frankincense may help. Read Spiritual writings to remove a demonic influence. This affliction may have come from a previous life.

Female Goblin (Hadar)

Female Goblin (Hadar)

The hierarchy of Female Goblins is fourth in the ascending rank of the dark energy ghosts, and they work under Jakhins. Their strength is around one thousand compared to a common ghost's strength of one and very low.

About two percent of the world's population is affected or possessed by the Female Goblin.

A Female Goblin will have a very strong odour, and the smell of a rotten egg is predominant.

A Female Goblin will not possess a person by entering the body. They can make things disappear by using a mantra. A female goblin's purpose is to acquire materials for black magic rituals, such as bones, skulls and digging up bodies from cemeteries for the subtle sorcerers.

To get relief from the influence of a female goblin, you can chant the name of God or the name of your higher source as to your religious belief. Chanting God with a higher level of spiritual practice will enhance your protection.

Female goblins give Jakhins information on dead people.

Jakhin

Jakhins are the fifth level ascending the hierarchy of the dark energy ranking. They make up about two percent of the world's population and have a strength of one thousand. Their strength is the same as the Female Goblins, and the Jakhins rank higher in the ascending ranking. The female goblins work for the Jakhins.

Jakhin can tie up and assume control over subtle bodies with their expert knowledge of mantras. Jakhins select the subtle bodies they desire and have them do various jobs to advance them based on their behaviour when they were alive on earth.

To get relief from the influence of a Jakhin, you can chant the name of God or the name of your higher source as to your religious belief. Chanting God with a higher level of spiritual practice will enhance your protection.

A spiritual healer has to have at least twenty percent more spirituality them the ghost to help the person affected by a dark energy spirit.

Some of the afflictions that people have may be coming from a previous lifetime.

Black Serpent (Kala Nag)

Black Serpent (Kala Nag)

The Black Serpent is the Snake Spirit. It ranks third in the hierarchy of dark energy and the ghostly realm. The spiritual strength of the Black Serpent is around one hundred. Only ten percent of the world's population is affected or possessed by the snake spirit. Ten percent remains a relatively low percentage compared to the common ghosts, and demons (rakshas) population affecting the world.

Keep in mind a ghost can take up any shape to achieve its objectives.

The percentages are a rough guideline that researchers have implemented over the years.

The black serpent's colour is green. However, the green colour distinguishes the Black Serpent from Yellow Serpents or snakes. The Black Spirit is called the Black Serpent Spirit because it consists of negative and dark energy.

A yellow snake spirit or Yellow Serpent denotes positive energy and qualities.

The Yellow Serpent will help humankind when they are spiritually seeking God and bringing good to humans and the earth.

Whereas the Black Serpent will use its dark energy to cause harm to humans and the earth.

A Black Serpent is always engrossed in its work, and they are short-tempered, shrewd, extremely smart and deceptive. The Black Serpent has many superpowers. Black Serpents are extremely aggressive to the point that their superpowers expel their dark energy quickly. The Black Serpent works under the orders of subtle sorcerers and mantriks.

Their spiritual practice is persistent and tremendously meticulous. They can gain access and take over a person's seven chakras. The seven chakras are in the human body, and the Chakras start at the base of the spine and run straight up the spinal cord until it ends at the crown of your head. These chakras are the central point of a person's body where your spiritual energy and your life force flow through. With spiritual practice, a person can become more attuned with their spiritual enlightenment to their highest evolution. This spiritual energy is known as Kundalini yoga.

A person under the influence of a Black Serpent can use this remedy to get rid of this dark influence. Increase your spiritual practice and direct more intense attention to your blocked chakras.

For a Spiritual Healer to effectively remove the dark energy from an affected person, they need twenty percent more positive energy than the Black Serpent.

Positive spiritual energies will make a person feel and look better, only for a short time.

A person can carry over the black energy from a Black Serpent from a previous lifetime.

The distress and affecting energy are more intense.

A spiritual healer may be of great help, and if the healer uses chanting as part of the healing ritual, recovery may be more expedient. An affected person is advised to maintain an ongoing spiritual practice to keep the Black Serpents' energy at bay.

Witch

Witch (Chet kin)

Witches have the spiritual strength of one thousand, and Witches affect about two percent of the world's population.

When a spirit of a Witch is near or in your presence, you will smell a foul odour.

A person possessed by a witch has a very loud laugh, and they will laugh continuously.

Witches can assume many different forms and cause accidents.

A Witch can enter a person's body and take control of their subtle body to get the person's body to work for them. Witches train the people they possess to perform dark energy rituals.

A person possessed by a Witch can take over a whole house. This possession will devastate and consume the family.

Witches are very well-versed in casting spells, mantras and tantras.

Witches work alongside the subtle sorcerers (mantriks), and they are the highest type of ghosts.

To rid yourself and your family of possessions of this type, you need to do a physical and spiritual cleansing of your house with special remedies and rituals.

Chanting the name of God or your Higher Source as to your religious background will be needed. Raising and enhancing your spirituality will help you rid yourself of this affliction and keep it at bay.

Using a spiritual healer, the healer will have to have twenty percent more spirituality than the ghost they are trying to abolish.

This type of possession could have come from a previous lifetime.

Spirits (Cheapish)

Spirit (Cheapish)

A Spirit has the strength of ten thousand verses the Common Ghost strength of one. A Spirit affects four percent of the world's population.

A Spirit will possess a human body, so they have somewhere to inhabit. A Spirit of this kind is very lazy, and is unlikely to cause real distress to the person and the person's body. Once a ghost inhabits a person's body, it can live there for many years. Devils, Demons, and other dark entities come, and go at will or will come and go continuously. Even after the death of the person they have inhabited, the Spirit will latch on to the subtle body.

When a Spirit possesses a person's body, the person's body will change in appearance. Their hair and body will take on an oily appearance. They will have a pale complexion, and their eyes will have a dull look. Any distress that is caused to the person's body will increase at night.

The Spirit will absorb the possessed person's digestive juices for food, and reduce the person's vital energy. The Vital energy called Prana-shakti decreases the possessed person's resistance, and they will fall ill frequently.

The possessed person will manifest signs of a twinkle in their eyes.

When others touch the possessed person's hands or feet, they will feel a sensation of pinpricks. Fingers, toes and the nails on them will manifest a long and pointed appearance.

To banish a Spirit from a person's body, the person will need Spiritual Healing. Some Spiritual Healers use musical notes of a specific combination, and the music is used to remove the Spirit of dark energies from a possessed person's body.

When the Spirit attacks a person, the Spirit will emit a dark black energy mist with a rancid oily smell. The putrid smell will distract the person and cause nausea and vomiting.

Using a Spiritual Healer, the healer will have to have twenty percent more spirituality than the ghost they are trying to abolish.

Often, a Spirit attachment of this kind can be from a previous lifetime. The dark energy Spirit has the reluctance to let go.

Black Coverings and Spiritual Cleansing

What is a black covering?

A black covering is an unseen energy that covers one's body without the person knowing it. This black covering can present itself in various ways and is very hard to detect. Many spiritual believers believe in black coverings. The black cover over a person's body is only detectable by someone with the psychic abilities of the six senses.

However, there are many physical and psychological signs which can indicate that a person may be affected by a black covering.

The symptom of pressure sensation is problematic and should be dealt with as soon as possible.

1. The person may feel a heaviness in some areas of the body. The pressure of something weighing the person down, the weight of a blanket completely covering you, and you cannot remove it.
2. There could be a feeling of sluggishness.
3. A covering on the head or the heaviness on the crown of the head. The person will have symptoms of not understanding, and cannot make decisions for themselves, and have feelings of confusion.
4. People have reported that they had the sensation of a covering in front of their eyes. Some people have complained about having a feeling of a veil over their face. Blurred vision for no reason is another indication of a black covering. The sensation of a tight band around the head is another common complaint.

5. If the covering is on the person's chest, they may have the sensation someone is trying to obstruct the person's breathing or have chest discomfort.
6. When a spiritual person encounters a person with a black covering, that person will have trouble seeing the person's face. The person with the black covering over his face will have a hazy look.
7. When a person is up close to a person with a black covering, the person will feel a subtle pressure, nausea and a foul smell.
8. Symptoms can present themselves on one side of the body, the upper top or lower half of a person's body, or the whole body wrapped in a blanket. The feeling of a blanket can be very thin or have a heavy rubbery texture.

People with a strong sixth sense will be able to detect the black covering by sight (the psychic ability of clairvoyance) and by feelings such as touching and sensing the vibrations (the psychic ability of Clairsentience). A person with the six senses and higher spirituality will be able to detect the affected person with a black covering.

Ways to do a Spiritual Cleansing:

Spiritual Cleansing is easy for most people. Spiritual Cleansing is imperative. A person should do a Spiritual Cleansing frequently.

Reading Holy Text is effective. Read the Bible. Charge the book with incense or charge the book in the sun for thirty minutes, then read the text from the book to help remove a black covering.

1. Cleanse your body with daily showers or baths. Baths and showers do more than take off the daily grime. They can wash off all the negativity you encounter throughout the day. The negativity comes from co-workers, family members, and people in public you have seen or you had interacted with. Daily baths and showers will help keep your aura clean and healthy.
2. Salt baths are a powerful and effective way to remove black coverings of negative energies.

Some researchers advise if a person is seeking relief from this type of darkness, use rock salt or sea salt in their baths. Some people use sea salt and crystals in their baths. Many people burn incense and use scented candles in the bathroom when taking their salt baths.

Note if you have crystals make sure they are water and salt tolerant.

3. Cleanse your home. Lightly spray a salt and water mist in every corner and room of your house.
4. Go around smudging your home. You can buy smudging sticks on amazon, or at a nearby specialty store.

Warning smudging with sage will rid you of all Spirits, including family Spirits.

5. Meditate, chant, pray and sing. Whatever is your spiritual preference. Chant the name God with spiritual emotion to generate positive energy. Chanting God helps to destroy any black covering, and you can do it anytime, anywhere and frequently.

Some meditators will chant these other names of God.

1. Shri Gurudev Datta
2. Om Namo Bhagawata Vasudevaya
3. Shri Durgadevyai Namaha
4. If there is no relief after one month, move on to the next name of God until you get relief. It is like going to the Doctor. When one medication does not work, move on to the next. Consult with a Spiritually evolved person.
5. Change your outlook on life. Be positive. A dark entity does not want you to be happy. If you are happy, they are losing their hold on you.
6. If all this fails, seek help from a professional, a Spiritual person, a Spiritual healer, your place of worship or a Preacher.
7. Find ways to be more Spiritual to raise your Spiritual vibration. The more spiritually enlightened you are, the less likely you will come under an attack from dark energy.
8. Change the company you keep. See your friends or family members less. By trying this, you will be able to figure out who the person is that has this influence on you, and makes you feel this negative energy.
9. Use your hands as if you are tearing, grabbing at the black cover and throwing it away. Our fingers and palms of our hands emit Pranshakti, or the Vital Energy needed to assist with removing the black coverings. If the black cover extends over a large area of your body, you start to remove the Black Covering from the bottom and work your way up to the top.

10. Your Chakras are the vital energy points of your body, and you need to clear them of blockages as soon as possible.
11. Use Spiritual Incense Sticks, light them and wave the smoke in the air, then all over your body. Do this practice once a day. Relief should come within a month.

You can perform this practice five to seven times a day. You may get relief within ten days.

If one scent of the incense stick is not working, move on to another scent.

SSRF has used scans to see if this method of incense works, and they found some evidence that it does have a favourable outcome.

12. Gomutra (India's Cow's Urine) is a highly Spiritual remedy used to wash inanimate objects. People use a few drops of urine in bathing to remove black coverings.
13. The use of the sun to remove a black covering. Go outside and stand in the sun for fifteen to twenty minutes every day. The best time is the morning sunlight. Make sure to do the back and front of your body. Ten minutes per side is sufficient.

Here is a little prayer I came across when I was doing research.

"O God, by your grace, let me be able to remove the distressing subtle black energy covering my body properly. Let no one in the vicinity is affected by the covering that I am going to remove. May the distress caused by the negative energies that I am suffering from be removed at the earliest."

"A prayer of gratitude should be offered right after this one, or work the things you are grateful for into this prayer."

Chapter Six

History of Cards Used for Fortune Telling

Fortune Telling Cards have been around for a great many years. Cards are said to predate the Pyramids by many centuries.

The Egyptians were the first to use a set of cards for Fortune Telling.

First came the Book of Hermes predated the pyramids by many centuries. The cards have beautiful embossed gold leaves and numbers resembling the Book of Thoth.

The book of Hermes is now known as the Hermetic Book of Destiny.

The Book of Thoth escaped the fires of the libraries that contained the purest doctrines of many profound subjects. The book housed many Egyptian secrets. These secrets were sought after by any Nation for their valued work.

The Book of Thoth became the reference to build the foundation for The Way of the Cartouche, an Oracle of Ancient Egyptian Magic. This mode of fortune-telling was to integrate the new with the old.

1. Level Spiritual, Transpersonal, or Superconscious.
2. Level Psychological, Mental or the Subconscious Level,
3. Level Material, Mundane or Conscious Level. These cards can be used for meditation and as a talisman.

This way of foreseeing the future was to be a way to solve the problems of the world.

A series of plates engraved with hieroglyphics containing numbers, letters, and pictures were used to design the cards. The meaning of the cards and the interpretation of what they meant to the person using them was determined by what game they played. The cards have different meanings to different people.

Some people played ordinary games with the cards. Other people used numbers, images, and letters to tell the future. These Cartouche Cards are not to be confused with Tarot Cards. These cards are a separate mode of divination.

In the Middle Eastern World, the Book of Thoth resurfaced. The book was known as the Book of Taro or Tora.

In the fourteenth century, a deck of cards held 52 cards. The cards were for playing games and not for telling the future. There was an addition of four court cards which increased the card deck to 56 cards. The deck consisted of 40 Minor Arcana and 16 court cards. Then with the addition of the 22 Major Arcana Cards the card deck increased to 78 cards in a Tarot deck.

Many ancient societies would like to take credit for the invention of fortune-telling cards. No one knows who was first to introduce playing cards to the people of their country. The people became very intuitive. People used their imagination, or was it their Psychic Abilities? They were able to use the cards to predict the future.

The Chinese used copper and silver plates engraved with designs, numbers, and pictures based on the four suits to make up the cards. They were the first to reproduce the cards using these plates on paper to make the first paper deck of cards.

It is said. Indian people also had their versions of the Tarot Cards. The cards held Hindu deities such as Swords, Sceptres, Cups, and Rings.

Ireland, Japan, Korea, North and South America, and the Pacific Islands also had their version of the Tarot cards using Swords, Sceptres, Cups, and Rings.

Egypt is still in the forerunner of the invention of fortune-telling cards.

These cards made it into Europe around the eleventh century and 1200 AD, in the way of traversals and trading goods with many countries. Some sources said the Egyptians corrupted the Saracens or Gypsies.

The Gypsies brought the cards with them when travelling from country to country. The Head of State and the Church sanctioned the cards for their abilities to see into the future.

The Knights of Templar brought the cards back from one of their crusades to the Holy Land. The Gypsies showed the Knights how to play the cards. The Synod of Worcester forbade the Knights of Templar to use the cards.

Until the fifteenth century, the cards were banned and sanctioned by the Heads of State and the Church. These cards became the rage of Europe. The cards were used as a pass time until the cards proved to be of use to foresee the future.

In 1390 Charles the VI was deemed mentally disturbed, and his wife Odette was given a deck of cards from a Templar. She did not think the cards were cheery enough, so she had a court artist draw pictures on the cards. She presented the cards to her husband and encouraged him to play with them. His mental condition improved so much that he resumed his duties.

Odette found that cards could bring in revenue by selling the cards throughout the Kingdom.

A Gypsy heard of the Kings' interest in these cards, and she made herself available to Odette. She showed Odette how to use the cards for their powers of prophecy. In no time, the entire court was using the cards to uncover political plots and hatch new ones.

Eventually, the King banned the cards from the Kingdom. The people of the Kingdom did not welcome the ban on the cards. Charles VI and Odette called on the Court Artist to have another set of cards drawn depicting mythological gods and goddesses, biblical characters, historical and national heroes, himself, Odette, and many court members. In no time, the cards were in use throughout the courtyard, Paris, and France.

Four hundred years later, Napoleon planned and won many battles using these cards to predict the future.

Back in England, as early as 1463, King Edward IV passed a law which forbade any importation of these cards into the country. The King was all for the use of the cards his country produced. The Church wanted the cards banned for good.

The cards were well established before Elizabeth I (1558 – 1603) took reign. The cards were used for political strategy and to gain personal victory over opponents.

Royalty used the cards to foretell the future. The cards played a big part in building the foundation of the British Empire.

Elizabeth 1st took the advice of her trusted adviser John Dee, and she called for the Execution of her half-sister Mary Queen of Scots and her husband, David Rissio. After the Execution, the cards were not used by Royalty for strategic plans to rule the British Empire. The cards were still in use for pleasure only.

In the Victorian Era 17th Century, The Church deemed the cards as an instrument of the Devil. The Church was calling for all cards to be out-lawed for good. The cards brought out man's worst traits in the way of gambling. When people used the cards, they thought they were promoting drunkenness, bawdiness, and sex. This attitude persisted well into the 20th century. Many homes to this day do not allow the use of cards.

Gypsies had a reputation for unworthiness. The cards still denote the image of the vagrant in the South of France even to this day.

In 1939 – 1945 Second World War, the cards regain the original appeal of a mystical purpose. People consulted the cards often in search of guidance.

The Tarot Cards have had many pictorial differences over the centuries. Most decks are used for fortune-telling and have the same basic meanings.

Swords are associated with Air.

Wands or Staves are associated with Fire.

Rings or Pentagrams are associated with the element Earth.

Cups are associated with the elements of Water.

The face cards are also associated with the element of Earth.

Page with Earth, Knight with Air, Queen with Water, and the King with Fire.

In conclusion, the cards were invented in Egypt all those years ago. They have kept their appeal and maintained their original meanings, century after century. The pictorials of the cards may have varied throughout the years.

The Fortune-telling cards were invented most likely by highly sensitive or Psychic People. Psychics use Tarot Cards as a visual tool of the trade. The more Psychic and intuitive the reader, the more reliable the readings are.

Here are Five versions of Tarot Cards to see how each foretells the future.

The Fool Card number 0

1. Aquarians Press. The card's prediction is an Optimistic, fresh start, Fun, Light-Hearted, Innocence, and In Search of Experience, Fulfillment.

2. Philip Permutt, New Beginnings, Spiritual, Traveler, Open to New Ideas, Fun, Adventure, Rushing in.
3. Sasha Fenton, Optimistic, Fresh Start, Fun, Light-Hearted, Rushing In, Adventure.
4. Arthur E. Waite, In Search of Experience, Travel, Fresh Start.
5. Sylvia Browne, Aspiration, Toward Limitless Potential.

The Sun XVII

1. Aquarian Press, Confidence, Success, Celebration, Joy, Triumph, Pleasure.
2. Philip Permutt, Success, energy, enlightenment.
3. Sasha Fenton, Joy, Happiness, Success, Fun.
4. Arthur Waite, Innocence, Wisdom, Nature, Art.
5. Sylvia Browne, Fixed, Unbiased, all-embracing, Nurturer, Objective.

I think the first four are very similar in prediction. The interpretations were based on Arthur Edward Waite's mode for predictions to tell the future.

Every Psychic may interpret the cards differently when they do a reading.

Now with Sylvia Browne's Interpretations, I see there is a difference. I believe she uses her intuition to interpret the cards. Sylvia Browne does use Arthur Edward Waites's philosophy on the Tarot Cards. Sylvia Browne has her own Spiritual Oracle Cards, in which she used her intuition to create her cards.

All information gathered here is based on all the Fortune Telling Psychic Books as a list by Author.

Aquarian Press, Deck of Cards, and pamphlet.

Philip Permutt, The Crystal Tarot Deck and Book

Sasha Fenton, Fortune Telling by Tarot, Beginners Guide

Arthur Edward Waite, The Pictorial Key to the Tarot Guide

Sylvia Browne, Phenomenon, The Secret History of Psychics, Books.

Divination

What is Divination?

Divination is many ways of searching the unknown for answers to questions about the future. Divination has been in use since the beginning of time.

People have always been curious about what the future holds. In search of these answers, people have used many devices to acquire a hopeful outcome to their questions.

Most people that use these divinations are self-proclaimed psychics, fortune tellers, priests, witches, shamans, healers, soothsayers, and exorcists. Every culture has a mystic way of treating the ailing by well-meaning practitioners. Not all these practitioners are legitimate though there are frauds in any field trying to make money.

Divination practices come in many forms. Listed here are some of the methods of Divination and Devices:

Alchemy was born in ancient Egypt as a way of fertility in the flood plains around the Nile. The Egyptians believed in life after death.

The Egyptians acquired a rudimentary knowledge of chemicals. They used chemicals to preserve the body. The chemical procedures gained through this practice gave the Egyptians hopeful insights into their search to live forever.

Taoist Monks pursued the search for an elixir for the inner and outer use of the body by using minerals of plants and other things, which could prolong life in humans.

People use the serum while doing exercise techniques like Qigong. Qigong is an exercise practice many people do to manipulate the chi. The chi is also known as the life force of the body.

In the Arabians' belief of metal, metals that contained mercury, and Sulphur were inferior, and gold was much better quality and a preferred metal. The Arabians thought the metals were able to be transmuted into gold. The substance was later to be known as the Philosopher's Stone.

The Chinese referred to the substance as the Pill of Immortality. Stones are in use for their divining power and properties for healing. The Philosopher's Stone in the Harry Potter book believes the person having possession of the stone will have Immortality.

Aleuromancy is used to tell the future by looking through flour, cakes, and powdery substances for signs. Another way to use Aleuromancy is to write the predictions on paper and then bake predictions in cakes, etc. The most famous known today is fortune cookies.

Astragyromancy divination will help you foretell the future using dice or bones with markings written on them with letters or numbers. Originally the dice were knucklebones. Knucklebones came from small bones of quadrupeds. People around 500 BC used bones or dice at funerals and religious sites. Archaeologists unearthed Astragalus's bones on an archaeological dig near the Altar of Aphrodite Ourania, near Athens, Greece.

A Diviner would shake the bones in a bag, then empty the bones of the bag on a table or the ground. The Diviner added the numbers or letters up for the prediction.

In the Tibetan Buddhism culture, the Dalai Lama used dough

balls and inserted pieces of paper into the balls with inscriptions. He uses the dough balls method for foretelling his future and used it for making everyday, and for important decisions.

Botanomancy divination is the art form of burning branches of trees and herbs. Then you interpret the signs and patterns in the smoke and flames. The person would decide which course of action he would be taking to avoid catastrophe. Predictions of Omens are forecasted this way as well. Most often used were branches of Brier and Vervain.

Capnomancy and Libanomancy are used to do readings by looking at the movements of smoke. Native Americans use this form of Capnomancy as a way for predictions. A thin and straight plume of smoke indicates a good omen. If the plume of smoke is large, it predicts the opposite. It was not a good omen for the smoke to touch the ground. You would have to take immediate action to avoid a catastrophe.

Capnomancy was used in Religious Ceremonies using cedar branches or shavings and burning animal sacrifices.

Today Capnomancy is burning cedar sticks, incense, and candles with ribbons tied around them. Sometimes the smoke is manipulated by the practitioners reading the shapes of the smoke.

Ceraunoscopy divination is by predicting signs in the sounds of thunder and lightning in storms. Ceraunoscopy is a form of Aeromancy.

Daphnomancy is a form of Pyromancy by burning bay and laurel leaves and listening to the crackling of branches when put into an open fire. The most commonly used are Bay and Laurel Leaves, etc. Loud crackling donates a good omen, whereas silence is a bad omen.

Dowsing using a forked stick or divining rod, looking for water, precious stones, and minerals. I know of one person who belongs to a Dowsing Group. The Group was out looking for Native Burial Grounds, and they found an Indian Chief buried sitting up with a full headdress and wearing native clothes of his culture. On the shores of Lake Erie. It was quite a significant find for the area.

Gyromancy is similar to the Ouija Board. There is a circle of letters drawn on the ground. The client goes around the circle, getting dizzy, then when the person starts stumbling on the letters. Then the letters are used to predict prophecies.

The dizziness is brought on by the spinning around quickly in the circle. This spinning intends to introduce randomness and facilitate an altered state of consciousness.

Ichthyomancy, Fortuning telling through interpreting the movements of live fish.

Metoposcopy predicts a person's destiny, character, and personality by reading the lines on one's forehead.

Molybdomancy divination uses the shape of lead it takes after it's poured into water. The cold moulted lead form is held up to candlelight and read. Other metals are melted and can be used in this method to predict the future.

Myomancy divination is observing the movement of mice and rats to predict the future.

Necromancy divination is predicting the future by speaking

to Spirits. Why would anyone want to talk with a Spirit or Ghost? One reason could be the Spirit, or the person may have unfinished business with the person they want to communicate with. Maybe, you do not want to let go of your loved one.

Many people seek out mediums who speak with the Spirit World. Some reasons for this are they want to know what is coming in the future. In my experience, Spirits are not supposed to divulge future events. Everyone is capable of speaking to a Spirit. A Spirit will talk to you telepathically.

Oneiromancy divination is being able to predict dreams. There are many books out there in the world that will interpret dreams for you. I interpret dreams by their narrative, how the dream's plot unfolds, and how it applies to me.

Occasionally, A dreamer transports to another time and place. On their return, they offer evidence of information to predict the future.

Ophiomancy is a way to predict omens by watching the serpent's behaviour through their movements of eating and coiling.

In Phrenology divination, the person interprets irregularities in the Cranium's shape. The indentations on the skull of someone's head can predict the character and mental abilities of a person.

Rhapsodomancy divination is when you open a sacred book, a book of poetry, or a book of spirituality, to find meaning in the message on the first line or paragraph of a randomly picked page.

Rhapsodomancy divination is a practice done in other ways. Another way is writing verses on separate pieces of paper and putting the pieces into a container. Then you pull one piece of paper out.

You read the prediction. Wood chunks can be used this way by writing verses on the wood. There are other various ways to gather predictions using this method.

Spodomancy divination is used by reading images in the cinders, soot, and ashes of a freshly extinguished fire for predictions. This method is exclusively not used in rituals.

Tasseography divination is when a person reads tea leaves, coffee grounds, and wine sediments to predict the future. I knew a person who could read all these particles, even the air bubbles in the foam of beer bottles after a person finished drinking out of them.

Other Methods of Divination

Astral travel is a way people travel around Spiritually without being aware of what is happening. The Spirit leaves the body for short periods. Astral travel usually happens after we have fallen asleep for the night. It is a way of travelling without paying for a vacation.

Our vivid dreams are unforgettable, and they are not dreams.

When you Astral Travel, everything in the dream seems so real, you have the feeling it was an unusual dream, and you remember every detail of the vision. It was not a dream your Spirit went Astral Traveling.

Victims of comas and debilitating illnesses astral travel frequently instead of staying inside their motionless bodies. The Spirit leaves the body, and it travels long and short distances for a short time. The Spirit returns to your body with a wakening jolt.

Astrology has been called upon to predict the future outcome of a specific time by using the positions of planets, sun, stars, and the moon's locations in orbit, by the month or year. Astrology is a way of predicting your horoscope. Astrology has piqued everyone's interest from ancient times to the present. People have always looked to the celestial bodies in search of answers.

An Aura is your life force and an etheric substance that surrounds everyone's body. Reading Auras is practiced by many. It is done by reading the energetic force field that emanates from the surrounding person. Everyone's Aura consists of colour bands of every colour of the rainbow, and the Colours of your Aura can tell you much about your feelings and health. Bright Auras are very good and healthy. Dark and murky Auras define ill health, dark entities, and feelings of depression. A person with dark auras can drain the energy of people with light Auras.

Crystal Balls come in different coloured crystals and different sizes.

A crystal ball should be used only by the ball's owner.

Use a crystal ball after dark. Your crystal ball should be placed on a stand, covered with a black cloth and kept in a cupboard to keep it clean and prevent fires. A crystal ball can pick up light sources and magnify the light rays and could start a fire. The owner of the crystal ball gazes into the ball in search of images that foretell the future.

Crystals and Gems accompany meditations for health reasons, promoting well-being and Spiritual enlightenment. Crystals are sometimes used with Tarot Cards and by some Psychics. Crystals can be used in balancing your Chakras and for opening the Third Eye, and Reiki for self-healing. Chakra and Reiki promote wellness and increase your Psychic Abilities.

Imitative Magic is an ancient form of divination practiced, and used by Native Americans, African Tribes, and Australian Aborigines. They use Imitative Magic by acting out ceremonial rituals in ceremonies. Some Imitative Ceremonies do not use ceremonial rituals. Some people performing rituals ask the gods and goddesses for what they need for survival. Rain dancing and calling for water are common in tribal ceremonies.

Infused Knowledge is passing information from one person to another without using the five senses. Infused Knowledge can come to you in dreams. A Spirit can communicate with you through telepathic thoughts. You want an answer to a question you have no prior knowledge of, and suddenly you know the answer.

Kinetic Energy is an unintentional, spontaneous manipulation of inanimate objects. These objects move by the energy created in a person's mind. A person can make these objects move without physical means. People use their minds to move things. Kinetic Energy can present itself in children and adults suddenly. It can present itself in times of great stress.

Kirlian Photography is photographs taken at night or in the dark to see a person's Aura. Kirlian Photography has been under great debate because it would be hard to prove that someone has not manipulated the photograph.

Numerology is a way to predict a person's character. When assigning a number to each letter of the alphabet, you only use numbers from one to nine. You add the numbers assigned to each letter of a person's birth name to get insight into a person's character.

Palmistry is a person who reads the palm lines of other people to predict numerous fascists of a person's life. Etc. The Heart Line, and The Lifeline.

Psychokinesis is known as Telekinesis. Someone with Telekinesis can move or manipulate objects without applying physical means or other scientifically explainable force.

Psychometry reads the vibrations of objects owned by other people.

Remote Viewing, a person can sit at home and see or visit another location spiritually.

Talismans, Crystals, Gems, and Cartouche Cards are all used as Talismans. People carry small objects on their bodies for symbols of good luck, health reasons, and many other reasons. It is up to the person and their superstitions what type of objects they prefer to carry.

Tarot Cards, the cards are read to foretell the future or to get an answer to a particular question.

Telepathy is direct transmitting or receiving a message through your mind without speaking out loud with another person.

Using Your Cards for Fortune Telling

When you buy your first deck of Tarot or Oracle Cards, pick up several decks if you have the option. See how the cards feel in your hands.

Do the cards have a good feeling?

Can your hands and your mind resonate with these cards?

Are you getting any intuitive impressions from the cards?

Do you feel vibrations? The vibrations make your fingers tingle, then that deck is likely for you.

Give the cards time to get accustomed to your vibration and intuition.

When you buy a Deck of Cards from the internet, Amazon, you still need to give the cards time to get accustomed to your vibrations and intuition.

The first thing you should do before using your new cards is to bless them and ask for protection from God. Ask the Holy Spirit to surround you with the white light and protect you from all evil and harm. You never know what or who is lurking around. It is better to protect yourself, even if it is only for your peace of mind.

After asking for protection. Knock three times on your cards to rid the cards of any negative vibrations. Do this every time you use your cards.

Taking out your cards for the first time is a little intimidating but exhilarating at the same time.

Rub your hands together to warm them up and get your vibrations working. Knocking three times on the cards neutralizes any negative vibes from previous readings. This method will cleanse the cards for your use.

Pray or meditate with the cards with a question in mind. Hopefully, you will receive the answer you are seeking.

There are many different ways to lay out your cards for readings. It does not matter how you place your cards or how many cards you use for a reading. Use what you are comfortable doing. There usually is a pamphlet in the card deck showing how to lay out the cards and their interpretations, or you can buy a book or check out card layouts online. It is all up to you and your intuition.

Handle your cards frequently and play with the cards. Use your intuition. Look and concentrate on the card. What is that card telling you? What are all the cards you laid out saying to you? The more you practice, the better you will become at doing readings. The impressions will come naturally and faster. Trust your intuition. Write a reading diary to later compare with the time frame of your question and the answer you received. Was the outcome in line with your reading or impression?

Have fun. Do experiment readings on your family and friends. Tell them it is only for practice and to have fun.

Be careful not to alarm anyone with bad vibes or interpretations from their reading. You will have to take responsibility for your interpretations. If anything is unsure in the reading, leaving it unsaid is better than miss interpreting it.

Maybe you will never use this skill, acquiring it for anything more than for yourself. You still have to be responsible for not alarming others.

Variation Card of the Day

The Variation Card of the Day card layout is used to get answers without a large card layout. I have listed several ways to get acquainted with your Tarot Cards. Practice makes perfect. If you are new to Tarot Cards, use the card of the day method. It will help you get familiar with your cards. Pull a card.

1. Meditate on your card, look at the card, remember the card, and study the pictures on the card.
2. What do you see in the pictures of the card? After studying your card, go with your first impression. It is usually the best one for you, and write down the impression in your Tarot Diary.
3. Do this exercise often. You do it in the morning or at night.
4. With keeping a Tarot Diary, you can refer back to it at any time to see your progress. Writing down your feelings or interpretation will eventually tailor your cards to your intuitions.

Choosing Your Favorite Card

Pick a favourite card. Your favourite card is not pulled from the card deck. You have to choose it. What does your favourite card say about you? Record your feelings in your journal.

Dream Card

A dream card is pulled from the deck rather than chosen. Record your dream card in your book and its significance to you. Update your dream card as your dreams change.

Stress Card

A stress card is a chosen card, and it is the direct opposite of your favourite card. Your stress card complements your favourite card. Your stress card will have negative feelings. This card will be the card you would not like to see turn up in your readings.

Card of the Unknown

The Card of the Unknown is a chosen card. Meditate on the card. Write down your impressions. Do you feel any vibrations from the card? Pay close attention to your impressions and intuition. These impressions can go a long way in future Tarot Readings. Record in a journal.

Future Prediction

Choose a card and write down your impressions. Put the card aside for a while. Take the card out and meditate on the card. Are your feelings and interpretations still the same as your original interpretation? Did the card predictions lead up to this day? Did your prediction come true?

Asking Questions:

Shuffle the cards. Hold the cards to your heart. Meditate on the cards by asking a question, then pull a card and interpret it. Record your interpretations.

Sample questions to ask cards.

How can I solve this problem? Why do I have this problem? Pull the outcome card.

Ask any question you want. Pull an outcome card. Pull another card if your card did not provide an answer, and keep pulling cards until you get answers and clarity.

Commentary Card

Shuffle your cards. Meditate and ask your question.

Pull Three Cards from the top.

Or Cut the Deck into three piles.

Pull the top card from each pile.

Interpret your card by your impressions or read the meaning in your interpretation book.

Write your impressions in your Tarot Journal.

Card One is your Present Situation.

Card Two is What is on your mind.

Card Three the background of today's events.

You use your impression, and intuition, or your book of Card Interpretations to answer your question.

The Internet has many layouts for card spreads and card placements.

Pinterest has many variations.

The sky is the limit. Everyone has methods of Tarot Readings. Make your own card layout

Past, Present and Future

There are many versions of this card layout.

Some people will lay the cards out in different ways by switching the cards around.

Knock three times on your cards to clear previous reading vibrations.

Shuffle the cards. Meditate, ask your question and record your interpretation in your Tarot Journal.

Tasks for the Day.

Card layout: 3, 2, 1

1. The card of the day.
2. The Specific Task for the Day.
3. Unique Chances for the Day.

Card layout: 2, 1, 3

1. The Situation.
2. The Past.
3. The Future.

Events for the Day

Card layout: 3, 2, 1.

1. Card one, The point for the day. What is important?
2. Card two is the outcome.
3. Card three, how does your day begin?

Another Layout to Consider:

Card Layout: 2 1 3

1. The Situation
2. The Past
3. The Future

Decision Making

Card layout.

Card 3 is in the upper left-hand corner.

Card 2 is in the right-hand corner.

Card 1 is under card 3 and card 2.

1. Card 3, What is your Situation?
2. Card 2, What is your Task?
3. Card 1, Is the outcome of your decision.

You can lay out your cards in so many different ways and ask any question you need an answer to.

You use your impression and intuition or your book of Card Interpretations to answer your question.

The Internet has many layouts for card spreads and card placements.

Pinterest has many variations.

The sky is the limit. Everyone has methods of Tarot Readings. Make your own card layouts.

The Celtic Cross

1. The Subject
2. Challenges.
3. The Goal.
4. The Distant Past.
5. The Recent Past.
6. The Near Future.
7. Subjects Attitude.
8. External Influence.
9. Inner Emotions.
10. Outcome.

Celtic Cross

The Celtic Cross is a favourite of mine. I use it most of the time.

The Celtic Cross will answer your question with more depth and insight. The version I use has three cards in the center overlapping. Instead of using ten cards, you use eleven cards.

If you happen to pull more than one card at a time, use all the cards at that placement in the reading. The extra cards will give you more information on that situation. I like the timing factor. You can use it to determine how much time into the future your reading will come to fruition.

The Timing Aspect:

You count your cards backwards from card number tenth or eleventh card, until you find a card with a digit in one of the suits, Cups, Coins, Swords or Staves. The number on the card will tell you the number of years, months, weeks or days.

For instance, if your first card going backwards is 10 of Swords, the timing indicated would be 10 months.

Coins cards indicate years.

Sword cards indicate months.

Staves cards indicate weeks.

Cup cards indicate days only if the card is next to a coin card.

For instance, if your card is 5 of cups and the next card in line is the 10 of coins, then your timing would indicate 5 days.

The Celtic Cross Picture

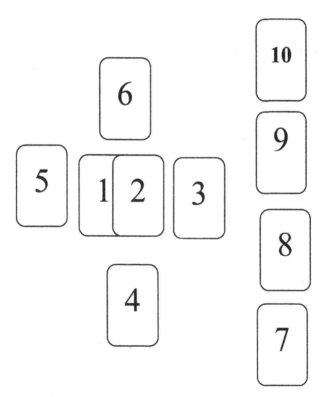

The Celtic Cross Variation

1. The Heart of the Matter.
2. The Challenges and the Issues at Hand.
3. The Unknown Influence.
4. The Past.
5. Your Hopes and Goals.
6. The Future.
7. Your Self-Image.
8. How Others See You.
9. Guidance and Warnings.
10. Inner Feelings, Hope and Fears.
11. Outcome.

The Celtic Cross Variation

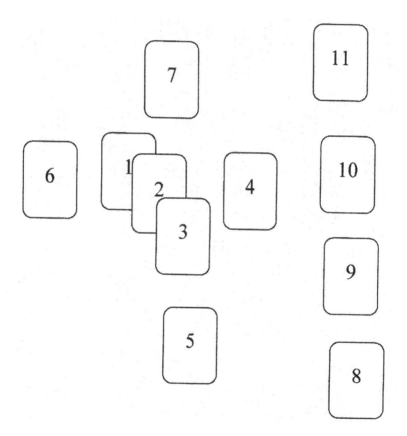

Six Card General Reading

The Card Placement for the Six Card General Reading is as follows;

Card 1	Card 2	Card 3
Card 4	Card 5	Card Six

You can use the 6-Card General Reading for many different readings.

You can write your version of the card layouts and jumble the cards up if you wish. Make up your questions and interpret the meaning of each of the cards.

There is no specific way for card layouts. Everyone is designing their card spreads. You can use this card layout to begin your readings until you get comfortable with your Tarot Cards.

Card One.   How do you feel about yourself?
Card Two.   What do you want most in your life at this time?
Card Three.   What are your fears?
Card Four.   What is working for you?
Card Five.   What is your problem and how is it holding you back?
Card Six.   The future or outcome.

15 Card Tarot Spread

1. Card Two is the Future.
2. Card Three is the Past.
3. Cards 13, 8, and 4 are What is the Outcome and not Immediate.
4. Cards 5, 9 and 12 are The Possible Near Future. What Affects You Now?
5. Cards 14, 10 and 6 are Advice, Warnings, And challenges.
6. The Cards cover Karma's Past Lives and how they Affect You now.
7. Cards 7, 15 and 11 Covers Your Future Outcome.

Fifteen Tarot Card Spread

| 13 | 8 | 4 |

| 5 | 9 | 12 |

What is the Outcome
Future

Possible Near

Not important

| 3 | 1 | 2 |

Past   Present Future

| 14 | 10 | 6 |

| 7 | 15 | 11 |

Advice, Warnings

And Challenges

Covers Future

Potential Outcome

Priority Card Spread

The Priority Spread is below, and the placement of the cards is as follows.

Card One. Upper left-hand corner.
Card One is for the Immediate Future, and it is Important

Card Two. Upper right-hand corner
Card Two is Important and not the Immediate Future.

Card Three. Lower left-hand corner,
Card Three is for the Immediate Future and is not Important.

Card Four is in the Lower right-hand corner.
Card Four is not the Immediate Future, and it is not Important.

Who Are You Card Spread?

1. Shoulders - The burdens this person carries/ the burdens they use to carry. You may need more cards to get the insight to this question.
2. The Heart - This is the core of this person. What is in their heart? What is their secret desire?
3. What Crosses the Heart - What this person had to endure? The challenges this person is facing.
4. The Spine - What supports this person and what keeps them going.
5. Hands - What the person is capable of. You will need more cards to get a better insight.
6. The Groin - Desires and wants.
7. The Feet - What the future holds and what path they are traveling on. More cards needed for more insight.
8. The Ground - The person's foundation.
9. Outside Influences
10. How the outside influences are affecting the person, or how the outside influences affected them in the past.

In a reading if the card in a certain position does not give clarity about the situation in question, pull extra cards to give you a more in depth reading on that particular area in the person's life.

Who Are You Card Spread

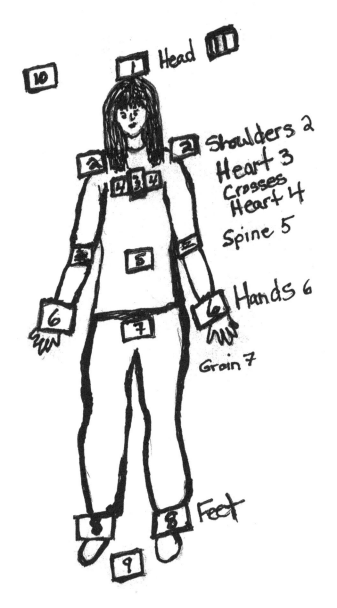

257

Reincarnation Card Spread

15 Card Spread, Your Previous Life

This Card layout is about your previous life. Who you were before you reincarnated to this life?

1. Who was I in my last life?
2. Was I married?
3. Was I happy in my last life?
4. What kind of work did I do in my last life?
5. Was I an honorable person?
6. What type of challenges and problems did I have in my last lifetime?
7. Was I a famous person in my last lifetime?
8. Did I have good health in my last lifetime?
9. How did I die?
10. Did I have a soul mate?
11. Is my present love someone I knew in my last life?
12. Am I linked to my parents of today from my last lifetime?
13. Are any of my family members of this lifetime from my previous life?
14. What do I need to accomplish in this lifetime?
15. Will I reincarnate after this present life?

15 Card Reincarnation Card Picture

The Tree of Life

1. Level of regeneration. My Ability for regeneration. The possibilities.
2. Level of creativity. My Inspirations. My Intuition.
3. Realization of Who I am.
4. Level of Occupation. Limitations and My Task. Attaining What I Need.
5. Social Level. My Kindness and Wild Naturalness.
6. Taming my Urges and My Self-discipline.
7. Spiritual Level. My Inner-self and Reflection. Seeking Spirituality.
8. Mental Level. My Feelings and Self-worthiness.
9. My Inner-self and Way of Thinking About Myself.
10. My Emotional Side. My Psyche and Unconscious Mind.
11. My Body. My Physical Being and the Environment Around Me.
12. Outside Influences.

Outcome.

Tree of Life Picture

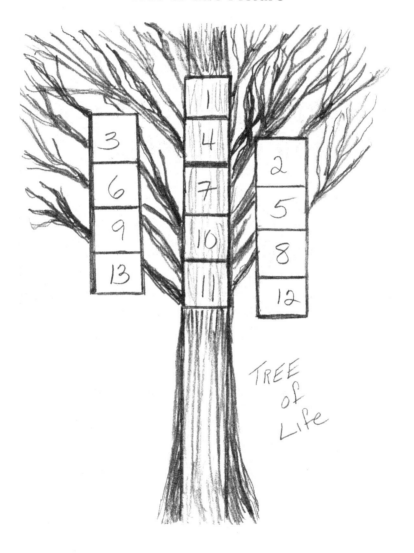

Chapter Seven

Astrology, Natal Charts and Horoscopes

Astrology, Natal Charts and Horoscopes are the same. There is no real difference when it comes to someone wanting to plot their life path. Each one of the headings uses a different name. The information gathered from the positions of celestial planets is used to make Natal and Astrology Charts. The people making the charts use the same method.

Natal Charts give a more in-depth reading when an Astrologer uses the exact time of birth.

A person's date of birth, place of birth, and time of birth are important information used by an Astrologer to construct the Natal chart.

Natal Astrology is also known as Genethliac Astrology. This astrology claims to provide information on a person's life path and personality. The exact time of birth is helpful for a more in-depth and accurate reading.

Once the information is collected, the interpretation consists of three steps. The first step is noting all the features in the chart. The second step is the process of chart weighting, plotting the planets by size and their distribution into the Zodiac Signs and Houses. The third step is Chart Shaping which involves accessing the placement of the planets by their aspects, and positions in the chart, and noting any specific patterns occurring between them.

Astrology as a whole is recognized as Pseudoscience by the Scientific Community. The statistical evidence fails to show any causation between the natal birth charts and the real-world consequences.

Natal Astrology has been around since the beginning of time. People from many cultures have counted on the position of planets to tell time. The locations of the planets help identify the seasons and to predict future outcomes. Each culture has its method of interpretation of the planetary solar system. They used their methods to predict the characteristics of people who may be compatible to work with and marry.

Sailors used the alignment of planets to navigate their ships when travelling the oceans.

In Hindu Astrology, the birth charts are called Kundalini, and they consult the charts to find out if a couple is compatible before marriage. The Hindu culture consults birth charts to predict auspicious events and rituals.

People of this generation put stock into the meaning of their Horoscope and Astrology by reading published books for the yearly forecast, reading their horoscopes in magazine and newspaper columns, they even have a daily prediction emailed to their in-box.

Even today, Astrology, with extensive research, has shown to have no existence of scientific proof. People still turn to astrology and horoscopes for insight into their daily lives. Researchers have found that it is possible to construct enough personality descriptions and generic aspects to satisfy people to maintain a large audience.

Astrology and the Natal Charts

Why would a Psychic need insight into their client's Astrological and Natal Chart?

Some Psychic Mediums believe the Astrological and Psychic Worlds are intertwined. Associating the astrological signs with the Five Senses plays a part in some people being Psychic.

We will take a quick look into this belief and how they are associated.

Psychics are turning to the World of Astrology to help with some of their readings. Usually, when this happens, the Psychic has had prior meetings with the client. The Psychic gets permission from their clients before they use Astrology. The astrological signs will give Psychic insights into the client's astrological life to give a more in-depth reading.

Since the beginning of time, people have used Seers (Psychics) and the cosmos to manifest their life. People from every walk of life, Pharaohs, Emperors, Kings, and Presidents, have looked to the Sun, Moon, Planets, and Stars for answers to their questions. People have plotted a chart to follow for this life on earth before leaving home on the Other Side. People can do this by using Astrology to help navigate their lives by foreseeing what options and obstacles are in their path.

Everyone knows of Astrology or the Zodiac and its composition of the ten Planets and the twelve Astrological Signs. These planets and astrological signs are designated Astrological segments of the calendar year.

Everyone has their comfort zone depending on the Sun's positioning in the universe at the time of birth.

Every sign has its personality and unique characteristic traits, tendencies and habits.

Our Sun sign determines the position of the Sun at the moment of our birth to form the Natal Chart.

Our Ascendant is also called the Rising Sign. The rising sign on the horizon when we are born is the essence, the spine of our character.

How Planet Signs Influence Our Characteristics:

The Sun and its position at your birth time symbolizes, and influence our Horoscope with these traits, vitality, vigour, stamina, and radiant energy.

Our Moon Sign is the position of the Moon at the time of our birth.

The moon sign is our personality and emotional makeup of people. The traits of the Moon are emotions, moods and instincts.

Mercury's position at the time of your birth will influence your character by increasing your intellect, the way you reason with decisions and how you learn.

Venus, Goddess of love, influences your character with these traits, love attraction and beauty. Venus will affect the way you attract your desires.

Mars and its dominating traits will influence your life and how you handle your aggression, desire, ambition, and passion. Mars will also determine how you act.

Jupiter will influence you with these traits, the growth in your life, your optimism and your luck.

Saturn is the planet that will influence your life through discipline, hard work and your structure in life.

Uranus will influence your life through your need for your freedom, making sudden changes, eccentricity and the rebellious side of your character.

Neptune will influence you with these traits, a mystic and intuitive mind, creativity and an artistic side of your character.

Pluto will influence the transformation and evolution of your life.

Now we have the four Earth Elements, which are triplicates.

The Air Signs are masculine. Libra, Gemini and Aquarius. Orientation towards their intellect.

Air signs deal with mental abilities and intellectual attributes.

Geminis, usually have ease of acquiring and using communication information.

Libras, weight, balance, and compare the information.

Aquarians, apply what they know to universal principles.

The Water Signs are feminine Cancer, Pisces, and Scorpio.

The focus on water triplicity is on emotion and the feeling of intuition and deeper Psychic levels of life.

In Cancer, this quality manifests around the home and family.

Scorpio, centers around issues that involve death, joint resources, sexuality and metaphysics.

Pisces, people, this quality is most evident in a deep connection to the unconscious.

Water signs are fruitful because they relate to fertility.

The Earth Signs are feminine and the practical signs among us, Capricorn, Virgo and Taurus.

Pragmatism manifests where the earth's planets are.

Taurus, has the practicality to show up as an ability to accumulate and manage material sources.

Virgo, this talent is evident in intellectual matters in the practical application and use of material resources.

Capricorns, are terrific organizers and managers of financial and material resources.

The Fire Signs are masculine and have tendencies toward ambition, Aries, Sagittarius and Leo.
Aggression and leadership characteristics are Fire Signs.

Aries, people are good at launching new projects and ideas.

Leos, excel at being a manager, CEO, and the central figure other people gather around.

Sagittarius, are often spiritual and philosophical leaders.

The Quadruplicates

The Cardinals Signs: Aries, Cancer, Libra and Capricorn.

These people are outgoing and social and initiate new projects and ideas. In their challenges, they often lack the endurance to see the projects to the end.

Mutable Signs: Gemini, Virgo, Sagittarius and Pisces.

These people are great at adaptability. Mutable signs react to new situations by adapting to them. Their challenge is that they can be changeable or malleable.

Fixed Signs: Taurus, Leo, Scorpio and Aquarius.

These people resist change and continue to act and react according to Fixed Patterns. They have persistence, but their challenge is inflexibility and stubbornness.

The Sister Signs

The Sister Signs are directly opposite and six signs away from each other.

These are the sister signs.

Libra and Aries, Taurus and Scorpio, Gemini and Sagittarius, Cancer and Capricorn, Leo and Aquarius, Virgo and Pisces.

The Astrological Chart and Houses:

Aries ruled with the Planet Mars. March 21 to April 19

Aries are both Impulsive and Compulsive. They are intensely loyal. They tend to keep proving the same point over and over again until they convince themselves and others of their intelligence. They are mortally offended if you turn your back on them when they talk to you. Aries dislike change, and they need their own space. Aries like to resist Authority and are ambitious and passionate. They have good instincts and are aggressive with fiery personalities. Aries has good leadership skills with high levels of energy. Aries's true nature comes out when confronted and challenged in any situation.

Taurus ruled with the Planet Venus. April 20 to May 20

Taurus rules the ascendant and the moon sign, which is also Taurus. Taurus is known for the triple Taurus. A Taurus says I am sorry a lot, and they can be boring to the fault. They have the chronic act of defense for attention. Their verbalization patterns tend to be either poetic or overly verbose. They can be slow to forgive, stubborn, artistic, and can care deeply for ecology. They like neatness. Taurus are not family-oriented but very protective of loved ones, sentimental about birthdays and anniversaries, etc. Taurus loves earthy pleasures and materialism. The Goddess of love symbolizes beauty and luxury. They seek sensual pleasure are the qualities of Venus.

Gemini ruled with the Planet Mercury. May 21 to June 21

Geminis are avid talkers. They are very cautious about forming friendships and relationships. Geminis are self-conscious, and they are very concerned with learning. Geminis can be changeable, multifaceted, fun, easy-going and yet fickle. Geminis are hard to keep grounded. Geminis are quick-witted, chatty and intrigued people by nature. Geminis have high intellect, and they love to socialize. The Mercury side of Gemini people analyzes everything.

Cancer ruled with the Planet Moon. June 22 to July 22

Cancerians are home-loving and protective of their families. They are animal lovers. Cancerians are intensively selective, prone to moodiness, but fight it, easily hurt, and like to repeat the same stories multiple times and never get to the punch line. Cancerians are highly emotional, caring, and empathic and are in touch with everyone around them. The Moon influences Cancerians through their emotions, feelings, and a general sense of comfort.

Leo ruled with the Sun. Jul 23 to Aug 22

Leos have great determination. They are insecure, have strong fidelity, heartbroken if hurt by someone, are enraged if a loved one is hurt, hate to lie, and hate liars more. Leos do not like hard work and are very fond of material wealth. They hate to lose. They do not like people to form their opinions themselves. Leos are more psychic about events than about other people.

Leos love to be the center of attention at any place or event. They are loyal, dramatic and have a generous nature. The Sun gives them radiant positivity, outlook and confidence.

Virgo ruled with the Planet Mercury. Aug 23 to Sept 22

Virgos have a prim exterior, are organized, meticulous and good translator-interpreters. Virgos are good with people, obsessive about colours and finishing what they start. Virgos like to make lists, are hypersensitive, faithfully in love, and can love more than one person at a time. Virgos are better supporters than front-runners in an organization. They dislike change and can be permissive but inconsistent parents. Virgos have a keen intellect and analytical skills with plans well executed. The Mercury side of Virgos is they can multi-task and can be quick-witted people.

Libra ruled with the Planet Venus. Sept 23 to Oct 23

Libras are natural mediators, and tend to jump from subject to subject when talking to someone. They are affectionate and generous but secretive, have bad tempers, and resent unsolicited advice. They love beauty and are empathic, seeing illness and self-pity as a weakness. Libras despise ingratitude. They are honest to a fault and seek equal balance and harmony in both sexes. Libras have an eye for beauty and are artistic. Libras try to be happy and have a fulfilling love life. Libras are romantic and love to share lots of love with being the Venus side of their character.

Scorpio ruled with the Planet Pluto. Oct 24 to Nov 21

Scorpios are goal-oriented and not prone to verbalize their thoughts. Scorpios would like to change the world to suit them. Scorpios like to cover all their bases professionally and personally. They love to take charge but move slowly. Scorpios are slow to battle and innately secure. Scorpios are loners and approach life with their own set of truths. Natural stamina comes easy to Scorpios, and Scorpios make great teachers. Scorpios are interested in life-changing transformations such as birth, death, creation and destruction. Scorpios can be eccentric with the Pluto influence.

Sagittarius ruled with the Planet Jupiter. Nov 22 to Dec 21

Sagittarius is very analytical and they love mind-involved issues. They are in constant need of validation and anxiety-ridden with quick wittiness. They love to postulate no matter what the subject. Sagittarius needs their space and freedom to do their own thing. Sagittarius is faithful and soft-hearted but capable of being vindictive. They can be blunt and to the point but highly intellectualized. Sagittarius are happy-go-lucky people who exude positive vibes around them. They have a thirst for knowledge and like to try out new things. Jupiter's influences are free Spirits, carelessness and optimism.

Capricorn rules with the Planet Saturn. Dec 22 to Jan 19

Capricorns have intellectualized emotions, love obstacles, are analytical to a fault, and are brilliant. Capricorns are retentive with their memories and don't tolerate phobias within themselves. They are great humanitarians and love helping others. Capricorns are not vindictive, and they will let bygones be bygones. They are flexible to others' opinions and will listen to all options before making a judgment. They are overly scrupulous about clothing and neatness with themselves. They are comfortable with their set patterns. Capricorns are disciplined, hard-working, and will not take shortcuts. They can be restrictive at times. The Saturn influences are tough to love and structure.

Aquarius ruled with the Planet Uranus. Jan 20 to Feb 18

Aquarians are natural-born teachers. They are more comfortable in group settings than one in one relationship. They love to dance and love the water and the ocean. They are introverts and extroverted at the same time. They slow to anger but are furious when they get there. Aquarians are romantic, very ingenious and hate injustice. Aquarians are brilliant, quick thinkers and prone to sudden changes. They are innovators with their innovative thoughts. Uranus influences the Aquarians through their rebellious side, and they are brilliant with new ideas.

Pisces ruled with the Planet Neptune. Feb 18 to Mar 20

Pisces thrives on compliments, not empty flattery, and they can tell the difference. They are deeply sensitive to slights and insults. They rarely suffer in silence when offended. Pisces need romance, not just sex in relationships. They are avid readers, students and note-takers. They are very stubborn and flexible if they are in the wrong. Pisces are great secret keepers, and they despise prejudice and bigotry. Pisces are quick to defend unfairly treated people.

Pisces is emotional and spiritual and have artistic traits. Pisces have high ambitions and want their dreams to be a reality. Neptune brings on the aura of illusions and poetic beauty.

The Astrological Houses:

Aries is in the 1ˢᵗ House:

Aries in the 1ˢᵗ House, this Astrological Sign is about anything new. The 1ˢᵗ House of Aries covers all first impressions, new beginnings, your-self image, and any new initiatives you undertake. Aries physically rules personal well-being. Early life, personality and physical appearance are other aspects of Aries.

Taurus in the 2ⁿᵈ House

Taurus in the 2ⁿᵈ House influences Finances, Personal Material Resources, Assets, Expenditures, and attitudes toward money. Taurus in the 2ⁿᵈ House also manages your immediate surroundings, smell, sights, sounds and taste.

Gemini in the 3ʳᵈ House

Gemini in the 3ʳᵈ House influences Communication, Intellect, mental attitudes, short journeys, brothers, sisters, neighbours and relatives. Gemini in the 3ʳᵈ House will determine how you interact in society as a whole.

Cancer in the 4th House

Cancer in the 4th House is at the bottom of the zodiac wheel. Cancer in the 4th House influences your Family Life, domestic affairs, Real Estate, Relationship with Mother and Father and early childhood conditioning, your roots and the end of your life.

Leo in the 5th House

Leo in the 5th House influences Children and Creativity, Pleasurable pursuits, creative outlets, particularly the firstborn children, love affairs, and sex for pleasure.

Virgo in the 6th House

Virgo in the 6th House influences your work and your health. Working conditions, environment, competence and skills and general health. Organization and discipline, Healthy Natural Living and being of service to others.

Libra in the 7th House

Libra in the 7th House rules Partnerships and all partnerships in general, marriages, open conflicts, and identification with others. Libra influences how we pick our Business Partners and Romance Partners in our Business and personal lives.

Scorpio in the 8th House

Scorpio in the 8th House influences Death and Inheritances fall under this dark House. The Occult, Transformations of all kinds, regeneration, sexuality, taxes, death, Psychic Ability and metaphysical aspects that Scorpio in the 8th House influences.

Sagittarius in the 9th House

Sagittarius in the 9th House rules the Higher mind, philosophy and Religion. The law, long journeys, higher education, publishing, foreign travel, interest, ambitions, in-laws, and relatives of your marriage partner and spirituality also are influenced by the 9th House.

Capricorn in the 10th House

Capricorn in the 10th House rules Careers, Professions, status, your mother and Father, worldly ambitions, public life, and people in power over you. Capricorn governs your general development in life.

Aquarius in the 11th House

Aquarius is the 11th House that influences your friends, Group associations, hopes and wishes, ambitions and goals in life, and your network of friends.

Aquarius is the 11th House that determines how you interact with teachers, friends, and society and is often a determining factor in our friendships.

Pisces in the 12th House

Pisces in the 12th House rules your unconscious, intuitions, confinement, and that which we have not integrated into ourselves. Karma also falls under this House. Pisces in the 12th House impacts these traits of self-sacrifice, escapism, old age, seclusion, and isolation. Pisces in the 12th House represents all loose ends that do not fall under other Houses. The 12th House is responsible for creativity in the arts because of isolation.

The Zodiac Chart

Name	Ancient Date	Symbol	Season	Mean Duration Days	Sun's Longitude on Entry	Sun's Declination on Entry
Aries	21 March To 19 April	♈	Spring	30.46	0	0.00
Taurus	20 April to 19 May	♉	Spring	30.97	30	+11.47
Gemini	20 May to 20 June	♊	Spring	31.33	60	+20.15
Cancer	21 June to 22 July	♋	Summer	31.45	90	+23.44
Leo	23 July to 22 Aug.	♌	Summer	31.29	120	+20.15
Virgo	23 August to 21 Sept.	♍	Summer	30.90	150	+11.47
Libra	22 Sept. to 23 Oct.	♎	Autumn	30.39	180	0.00
Scorpio	24 Oct. to 21 Nov.	♏	Autumn	29.90	210	-11.47
Sagittarius	22 Nov. to 21 Dec.	♐	Autumn	29.56	240	-20.15
Capricorn	22 Dec. to 19 Jan.	♑	Winter	29.45	270	-23.44
Aquarius	20 Jan. to 18 Feb.	♒	Winter	29.59	300	-20.15
Pisces	19 Feb. to 20 March	♓	Winter	29.71	330	-11.47

Twelve Card Astrological Spread

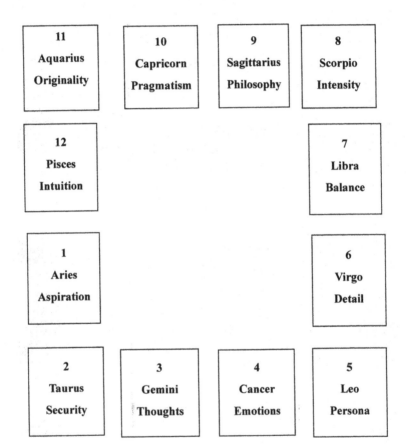

| 11 Aquarius Originality | 10 Capricorn Pragmatism | 9 Sagittarius Philosophy | 8 Scorpio Intensity |

| 12 Pisces Intuition | | | 7 Libra Balance |

| 1 Aries Aspiration | | | 6 Virgo Detail |

| 2 Taurus Security | 3 Gemini Thoughts | 4 Cancer Emotions | 5 Leo Persona |

Astrological Houses

When you work with the Astrological Houses you place your first card at the number nine placement on a clock. You go counter clock wise for the rest of the cards.

Card 1.   Is in the placement at 9:00. Self Appearance falls under the first House.

Card 2.   Is in the placement at 8:00. Finances, Possessions fall under the Second House.

Card 3.   Is in the placement at 7:00. Your Mind, Siblings, Neighbours, and Short Trips fall under the 3rd House.

Card 4.   Is in the placement at 6:00. Home, Family, and where you are coming from falls under 4th House.

Card 5.   Is in the placement at 5:00. Creativity, Children, Romance and Speculation falls under the 5th House.

Card 6.   Is in the placement at 4:00. Work, Health and Routines fall under the 6th House.

Card 7.   Is in the placement at 3:00. Relationships and Partnerships fall under the 7th House.

Card 8.   Is in the placement of 2:00. Sex, Death, Joint Finances, and Taxes fall under the 8th House.

Card 9.   Is in the placement at 1:00. Higher Education, Travel, Spirituality, and Philosophy fall under the 9th House.

Card 10.   Is in the placement at 12:00. Recognition, Honors, Careers and Fame full under the 10th House.

Card 11.   Is in the placement at 11:00. Your Social Life, Friends, and your Goals fall under the 11th House.

Card 12.   Is in the placement at 10:00. Karma, Secrets, Self-Doubt, and Hidden Enemies fall under the 12th House.

Astrological Houses Spread for the Year

The Cards and Definitions
For Everyday Life

House 1.	The Questioner, The Body and appearance. People closely affecting the Questioner if a Court Card falls here.
House 2	Money and Possessions, Values
House 3	Legal Affairs, Siblings, Neighbours, Education and Communication.
House 4	Home, Mother, Premises Both Home and Work.
House 5	Children, Amusements, Lovers, Enterprises, Speculations in either Business or Other Gambles.
House 6	Work, Service, Health, Hospitals, Bosses and Employees.
House 7	Partners, Relationships, Marriage.
House 8	Corporate or Shared Money, The Deep Side of Life, Birth and Death, Sex, Relationships where the sex is very important.
House 9	Travel and Foreigners, The Law, Religion, Mysticism, Higher Education, Outdoor Life, Horses.
House 10	Status, Career, Aims, Father.
House 11	Friends, Clubs, Intellectual, Hobbies.
House 12	Inner Self, Psyche, Inner Peace or Terror.
House 13	**Center Card for Luck or Outcome**

Health Spread

House 1	The Head, Eyes, Ears, and Upper Jaw, Inflammatory Conditions, and Accidents.
House 2	The Lower Jaw, Throat, Trachea, and Thyroid.

House 3	The Respiratory System, Shoulders, Arms, Hands, Brain, Nervous System, Glands.
House 4	The Chest, Breast, Alimentary Food System, Esophagus, Stomach, Gall Bladder, and Bile Ducts.
House 5	The Heart, Spine, Thymus, Endocrine Glands, behind the upper area of the Sternum.
House 6	Lower Intestines, Colon, Skin, Bowel, Internal and External Allergies of Nervous Origin, General Debility and Tiredness Due to worry or Over Work.
House 7	The Kidneys, Pancreas, and Bladder.
House 8	Gonads, Reproductive Organs, Formation of Cells.
House 9	Liver, Pituitary Gland, Hormone Production, Physical Growth, Weight Problems.
House 10	The Knees, Gall Bladder, Spleen, Skin, Teeth, Bones, Ears, Bone Muscle Structure.
House 11	The Lower Legs, Ankles, Circulatory System.
House 12	The Feet, General Nervous System, Respiratory System, Food Allergies, Mental Problems.
House 13	**Center Card for Insight.**

Astrological 13 Card Spread

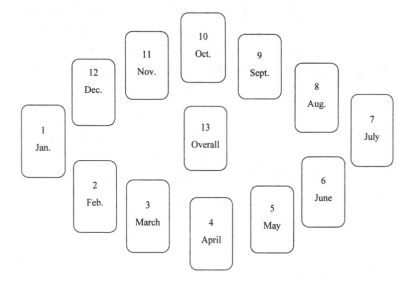

Oracle Cards Versus Tarot Cards

Both sets of cards will give the reader and the questioner Insight, Perspective, Clarity, Personal Growth, and Inspiration through Divination.

Tarot Cards were expensive, and each card was handcrafted. It would take the artist many hours to make one card. Only the wealthy could afford to buy the cards. The cards were scarce until the Head of the Countries employed an artist to make the cards. The Royal Kingdom thought the sale of the cards would generate income, and they created their own cards.

People will always want to find insight into their future by any means of Divination.

What is the difference between Oracle Cards and Tarot Cards?

There is quite a difference between Oracle Cards and Tarot Cards.

The Egyptians had their book of Thoth and their set of cards to gain insight into their future. The Egyptian Cards date back to the beginning of time.

Tarot Cards come from ancient roots dating back to the fourteen hundreds when they made their way into Europe. Tarot Cards have a structured set of rules. The deck has seventy-eight cards per deck. Which makes them almost the largest card deck with that number of cards on the market today.

Although that has changed recently, some new designers are designing Oracle Decks with more than a hundred cards per deck. Tarot Cards are predictable with their structure, and set of rules.

Each card has a specific meaning. Anyone who has used the Arthur E. Waite Cards and the methodology of the cards can probably use any set of Tarot Cards.

I have seen new Tarot Deck Designers taking this to a new level. The decks still have seventy-eight cards, but the themes are starting to change. Some designers think the old Arthur Edward Waite Tarot Decks are crude with their meanings, and pictures as they are.

This is where Oracle Decks come into the picture. The designers can make the Oracle Decks with more pleasing themes and interpretations.

Oracle Cards are newer than Tarot and have no specific structure. This is where the Designer has more control over the composition of their deck. The Oracle Deck does very well on the market today. They do give Tarot Cards a run for their money. I like both, and I do purchase both Card Decks. Designers are more creative now, and several different card decks are designed every day and sold on the market.

Each deck of Oracle Cards has their specific rules. The designer of their cards devises the rules to follow. Oracle Cards have many different themes, Angels, Fairies, Guides, Moonology, and many more.

Professional Card Readers use Tarot and Oracle Cards in their practice to validate the outcome of the reading. Tarot and Oracle Cards each have their own merits. The reader should always use their intuition with both decks. Oracle Cards are becoming very popular.

Oracle Cards come in various sizes of decks. The decks may have thirty-six to sixty-four cards per deck. The size of the decks depends on the Designer of the cards. Larger size decks are designed and sold on the market today.

Oracle Cards have the card's meaning written on them, and most do come with a booklet to let the reader know what the cards mean. The booklet that comes with the deck has the Designer's reasoning and insight for each card.

What is the better deck, Oracle versus Tarot?

No deck is the better deck. It is a matter of what you prefer.

The Oracle Decks I own have many different themes. The Tarot Cards I own are Arthur E. Waite, Waite and Riders Decks' original designs. I also have other Tarot Decks that follow the same structure and meanings as the Arthur E. Waite's design. I like them all.

Your intuitive mind is the key to reading the cards of any theme.

Oracle decks are easier to use because they have pictures and written meanings on each card. Oracle Cards usually do not have suits to follow, but they do have themes. Oracle decks have themes that go together like suits in the card deck. Suits in an Oracle deck may be new.

The Moonology Deck has different phases, where there could be different categories, like suits. Whereas, the Tarot Deck has four suits, Swords, Cups, Pentacles and Staves. That is a constant with Tarot Decks.

Tarot Cards take time to memorize all the meanings. They usually do not have the card's insight written on them. You have to consult the manual that came with the cards, or you may have to purchase a book to explain what the cards mean, how, and what card layouts to use.

Use Your intuition!

Numerology

What is Numerology?

Numerology is another method of Divination people use to predict or understand their composition. Numerologists implemented using numbers to unlock the mysteries of the past, present and future. Numerology is based on and present in most things we do every day. Divinations that use numbers to enhance the prediction of the past, present and future are Tarot Numerology, Astro-Numerology and Numerology in Chakras. Several more systems of Divination practices use numbers in their foundation of predicting the future.

Mystic Numerology, known as the Chaldean System, is the most common and popular system. Chaldean System is the Pythagorean Method. Pythagorean Numerology dates back to the sixth century and is considered the Father of Modern Mathematics. Pythagoras is known as the Greek Master of Mathematics and who also studied the Hermetic Sciences. Pythagoras taught both methods of Metaphysical and Scientific Numerology.

Numerology is the study of the number system, and each number has its vibrational frequency and meaning. Numerology has been around since the beginning of time. This ancient method of Divination may be prophetic. Numerology may be a way to unlock a person's psychic abilities.

People have always needed a way to keep track of everything, from counting livestock and understanding the cosmos.

A Numerologist use numerology to interpret the insight of a client's composition. The client's personality characteristics, and the spiritual path the person is working on in this lifetime.

Numerology is a system of numbers using numbers from 1 to 9.

Life Path

You use the day you were born, the month, and your birth year. You use your birth numbers to find your Life Path.

We will use birth date and year, for example, Jan. 31st, 1957. Jan. is the 1st month = 01 + 31 days + 1957

You reduce double digits to a single number.

You add the numbers up, 01+3+1+1+9+5+7=26. Now add 2+6=8

8 is the number of your Life Path. You then look at the interpretations of the numbers for Life Path 8.

There is an exception to the rule if your life path number happens to be 11, 22, 33, 44. These numbers are master numbers, and they have special meanings. Double numbers have a stronger vibration and amplification. Reduce the numbers to a single digit.

You have a life path of 11 and 2. You add the two ones together. You have the number 2 as your final number. Read as 11/2.

Life Path Interpretations

Number One

Number One is the strongest because it comes first in the number system. The number one is associated with autonomy, independence, individuality, new beginnings, and oneself. Positive Traits: a number one person is considered an Innovated Pioneer, Confident Planner, Independent, Proud, Self-confident, Imaginative, Courageous, Born Leader, Ambitious, Bold and Strong. Number One has to be noticed and usually presents itself as self-assured. They require excitement, adventure, and a love of freedom. Negative Traits and Challenges: Number Ones can be uncompromising, selfish, weak, critical, aggressive, egotistic, impatient, dominant, overprotective, defensive, opinionated and conceited. Number One is prone to be lonely and anger easy and needs the love and support of friends and family. Number One needs self-discipline and respect for others. Number One can be brutally honest.

Number Two

Number Two deals with duality issues. Positive Traits: Two's are balancing and loving people, caring, empathic, kind, gentle, tactful, indecisive, diplomatic, skilled at mediating stressful situations, honest, outgoing, funny, and adaptable. Number Two people are fun-loving and happy-go-lucky people. They are highly sensitive. Negative Traits and Challenges: lonely, needy, insecure, moody, fussy, deeply emotionally sensitive and submissive. They focus on negativity and criticism. They must stop seeking external validation and stand up for themselves. Overcome fear and find their potential. Number Two, people need their space when they are grumpy. They will lie to keep harmony.

Number Three

Number Three people are highly creative and need constant stimulation and socialization. Positive Traits: outgoing, funny, lucky, optimistic, friendly, entertaining, love communicating and gifted with words, cheerful in nature, highly motivative, energetic. They inspire others and make others happy when around them. Negative Traits and Challenges: Number Threes are scattered, superficial, extravagant, deceitful, and lacking in direction. They are shy and self-conscious about what people think of them. It is challenging for them to stay optimistic and realistic during tough times. Having trouble committing or focusing may tend to abandon the task. Number Three can be childish, gossipy, critical, and whiny.

Number Four

Number Four people keep their emotions and feelings hidden. Positive Traits: need encouragement to get out and socialize. Number Four seeks financial security, is faithful, honest, dependable, grounded, structured, orderly, practical, disciplined, and adheres to principles.

They are methodical and hardworking. They are into their healthy way of life. Negative Traits and Challenges: The Number Four are ridged and fixated on rules and regulations.

Irritated when others do not follow the rules. They have trouble balancing ambitions, and they need stability. Number Fours tend to be lazy, impatient, slow, rigid, and boring. Fours tend to be depressive, inflexible, soft-hearted and a pushover. Number Fours are often chaotic. They can find themselves in legal difficulties.

Number Five

Number Five is like a hurricane full of energy. Positive Traits:

Martha G Klimek

Needs freedom and room to breathe. They love communication, transitions and education. They can be flexible, intelligent, romantic, curious, impulsive, playful, sexual, witty, and adventurous they love to escape. They love to travel, find pleasure in the simplest things and are inquisitive. Negative Traits and Challenges: Number Fives feel restless and impatient due to their urge to learn new things. They find they have challenges with personal and professional relationships. Number Fives tend to be irresponsible, unstable at times, and like to be mischievous. Fives like being risk-takers for the excitement. They can be very demanding, and they get restless and bored quickly.

They are melodramatic at times. Moodiness, being hasty at times and tending to be sharp in their speech. They are self-indulgent and have difficulties with authority.

Number Six

Number Six is empathetic and resonates with family and responsibilities. Positive Traits: They like to be a service to others. Have a concern with relationship issues and emotions. They love harmony, peace, and home. They are nurturing, magnetic, managers, principled, idealistic and compassionate. They are careful and slow movers in life. They make great parents. Negative Traits and Challenges: Sixes challenges are to remain consistent, controlling, dominating, self-righteous, jealous, interfering, co-dependent, martyr, gullible, unforgiving and stubborn.

Number Seven

Number Seven has an imagination and introspection and loves to investigate with their analytical skills. Number Sevens have keen eyes and are observant. Sevens are inventive, quick-witted, wise and inquisitive people. Number Sevens are creative, rarely bored, and good at entertaining themselves. They are reflective, intuitive, intellectual, love nature, and Spiritual. Negative Traits and Challenges: Sevens can be aloof, detached, depressive, deceitful, sarcastic, mysterious, superiorly, loner, moody, and cynical. Sevens have trouble listening to their rational side, logical side, intuition and creativity. They can be disappointing. They can see flaws in everything. They are not shy about telling others about their imperfections.

Number Eight

Number Eight loves success, money and authority. Positive Traits: They are into attaining goals, power and achievement. They are honest, responsible, ambitious, energetic, and powerful visionaries. No one can tell them how to behave, are fun to be around and have deep emotions.

Negative Traits and Challenges: Do not show affection or emotions until they are good and ready. They are relentless, headstrong, tense, power-hungry, narrow-minded, controlling, ruthless, intimidating, weak, with financial problems and may have gambling issues. They have trouble making up their minds about when to take charge or delegate. They do know how to accept constructive criticism.

Number Nine

Number Nine has deep values and is unwilling to compromise for convenience. Positive Traits: acceptance, understanding and compassion Number Nines tend to be generous, idealistic, stylish, magnetic, multi-talented, powerful, forgiving, tolerant, intuitive, musically inclined, and can be loners, natural leaders, and perfectionists. They need unconditional love, and they make good artists and writers. Nines are sympathetic. Number Nine can be psychic but under-use their gift. Negative Traits and Challenges:

They do not get over a lost love easily. They tend to be overachievers and martyrs. Often you will see them sullen.

They have vast knowledge and act as a jack-of-all-trades, masters of none, domineering, quick-tempered, clinging to the past, overly emotional, demanding approval and can be nonspiritual. They have codependency in relationships, focus on the future, and must strive to balance reality and dreams.

Number Ten Refer to Number One.

Master Numbers

Number Eleven

Number Eleven. 11/2 Refer back to Number Two. Number Eleven is into spiritual awareness, enlightenment and philosophical talents. Find their psychic gifts under extreme circumstances. Will respond to people's personal needs, needs of society or humanity. Often learn life and compassion the hard way. Influences modern fashion, art or music. They can be inspirational, creative, visionary, mystical, and have great inner strength. Negative Traits and Challenges: They can have nervous tension and act fanatically. They can be extremists, seeking the limelight, and impractical.

Number Twenty-two

Number Twenty-two. 22/4. The Master Builder Refer back to Number Four. Number Twenty-two increases the vibrational energy of Four.

Intuitive and innovative assist with the transformation. Creative, long-term legacies, and power. Capable of extremely professional, personal responsibility and success. Very hard working, Intuitive,

Psychic, great inner strength. Leader of a large scale, power, and utmost integrity. Negative Traits and Challenges: Nervous tension, fanatical, misusing power, manipulative, mismanaging, and hypersensitive.

Number Thirty-three

Number Thirty-three. 33/6 Refer back to Number six. The extras of number Thirty-three are extra physical, extra sensitive, extra emotional, extra lustful, maybe have extra lovers, sad childhood or trying. Loves to explore relationships, conscientiously work and friends.

There is the belief the Numeric Field with the numbers one to nine is used to give insight into your reading. You have to take into consideration that Numerologists base your life cycle on this numeric scale. When you look at it this way, your life does not end in your ninth year. What happens next? The years of your life span are divided into three cycles. The first twenty-seven years of your life, from ages one to twenty-seven, are your youth years. In your youth years, you are gaining knowledge. Your second segment of this cycle is the years twenty-eight to fifty-six and is considered your maturity years. The third cycle ranges from fifty-seven until the remainder of your life are your wisdom years.

Every nine years, everyone starts a new life cycle. This life cycle can define and determine the timing of events in different aspects of your life.

The stages are like this:

Year One.   Starting new projects.

Year Two.   Finishing projects started in year one. Take some time to have fun.

Year Three.   Creativity, Pregnancy and new friends.

Year Four   Stabilize your finances, buy property, and watch your weight.

Year Five   Travel, rage, being silly, sexually alive.

Year Six   Love deeply, work on relationships, family and family problems.

Year Seven.   Go within yourself for self-reflection, meditation, prayer, gentle pursuits, seeking spirituality and guidance.

Year Eight.   Going out, making money and physical challenges, being yourself.

Year Nine   Is for Reflection on your life and work on your mind, body and soul. It is a time for being quiet and the construction of new challenges and changes.

Numerology focuses on the use of nine numbers. These numbers are 1 to 9.

Considering the Master Numbers 11/2, 22/4, and 33/6, you add the master number to get your Single digit.

There are many different ways to use Numerology to Find Your Life Path, Your Destiny, Your Personality and Your Heart's Desire. You will have to use the Alphabet Chart provided. Let us take a look at how to do this using Numerology.

1. Your Destiny Number. You use your birth name, the name on your Birth Certificate and the corresponding letters on the chart to find the numbers that go with each letter of your name. Add up the numbers until you break them down to a single digit. The single digit will give you your destiny number. Some people use their nickname instead of their

birth name. Read the passage to get insight into your destiny number. What is your true purpose in this lifetime?

2. Life Path is an example earlier in this chapter. Please refer back to it. Full date of Birth. Find the single digit. The qualities of your core need to be at their best to make the most of your time here.

3. Personality Numbers, again using your full birth name. You use only the value of consonants. Reduce the number back to a single digit. The outside world perceives you with the first impressions of you and how others may influence you and your personality.

4. Your Heart's Desire. Using your full birth name. You are only using the value of the vowels now. Double digits reduce back to a single digit. Deepest desires, Priorities of your soul. To be fulfilled, the wisest part of your essence has to be acknowledged.

Here is another list explaining what the numbers mean. The list is the more condensed version.

1. Zero is empty but whole. Zeros can be creative, scattered, and disorganized.

2. Powerful, and they are excellent leaders. good at innovating and could be stubborn, and resentful of Authority.

3. Sympathetic, helpful, appreciative, routine, excellent confidant, insecure, unambitious.

4. The Center of attention, more sensitive, can be vain and superficial.

5. The practical, steady, honest, excellent money manager, overly cautious, quick to lose temper.

6. Resourceful, optimist, funny, makes friends easily, loves anything new, opportunistic, irresponsible.

7. Diplomat, a peacemaker, loves beautiful things, chronic worrier.

8. Introspective, philosophical, has a mystical outlook on life, isolated, secretive.
9. Ambitious, materialistic focuses on power and success more than family and Relationships, self centered, thoughtless.
10. Number 10 is Number One. Humanitarian, generous, compassionate, idealist, egocentric, overly sensitive.
11. Number Eleven is Number Two, Powerful, dominating, inspiring, rigid, and unreceptive to others' ideas.
12. Number Twelve is Number Three vibrations are most amplified, qualities Multiplied.
13. Number Thirteen is Number Four, and the vibrations are more amplified qualities multiplied.

Number Twenty-Two, back to Number Four, vibrations are more amplified qualities multiplied.

Conversion Chart next page.

Numerology Conversion Chart

A	1	H	8	O	6	V	4
B	2	I	9	P	7	W	5
C	3	J	1	Q	8	X	6
D	4	K	2	R	9	Y	7
E	5	L	3	S	1	Z	8
F	6	M	4	T	2		
G	7	N	5	U	3		

Tarot Numerology

Number One: New Beginnings, Opportunities, Potential.
Number Two: Partnerships, Balance, Duality.
Number Three: Expressions, Groups, Growth.
Number Four: Manifestations, Foundations, Stability.
Number Five: Conflict, Change, Instability.
Number Six: Harmony, Cooperation, Healing.
Number Seven: Reflection, Assessment, Control.
Number Eight: Mastery, Accomplishments, Action.
Number Nine: Attainment, Fulfillment, Fruition.
Number Ten: End of Cycle, Completion, Renewal.

Tarot works in cycles of ten.

Double Digits are always reduced to single digits, a single number.

$15 = 1 + 5 = 6$
$10 = 1 + 0 = 1$
$22 = 2 + 2 = 4$

Chapter Eight

Stories

20 Highway

This story is from a few years back. My husband went on a trip with the Scouting Group. The Canadian Scout Jamboree was held in Calgary, Alberta that year.

My grandchildren called and wanted me to go get them and their friends. They wanted to come to my place while my husband was away for ten days. I was looking forward to some time by myself and that did not happen.

I went to the city to pick up the four children that morning, and for some reason, I did not want to go. I had a bad feeling.

I am uncomfortable when I get these feelings. I was scared to the point of shaking, and I was very nervous. The drive to the city was an hour there and an hour back.

I parked the car at my daughter's place. I was relieved. I went into the house, and I wanted to stay. I did not want to leave in any shape or form.

The children were getting impatient with me because I was stalling. That feeling of dread would not leave. About an hour later, I told the children to grab their bags, and I was ready to go home.

The four children grabbed their bags, and were out in the car before I knew it. I still could not shake this feeling.

We were on the road heading to my place; I drove up the mountain and took Highway 20, our usual route, and I started to shake even more to the point, I was almost in a state of panic.

I paid extra attention to my driving. Having the children with me gave me little comfort, but talking to them helped me stay calm. The children knew something was off, but I was not going to tell them I was afraid of getting into an accident.

I instinctively knew there was going to be an accident.

I could not decide on an alternate route to drive home. All I knew was I had to get off of Hwy 20. The roads were far and few between. I stayed on my usual route of going home. I still wanted to pull off the road. How long was this fear going to last? I was out of the city with four children in my car. Reasoning with myself, I could not just sit on the side of the highway and watch the traffic go by, so I kept going.

I had a vision of a car weaving and then coming into the lane I was driving in, and a dust cloud and car parts were flying all over.

I went a little further down the road. I did not see the car swerving. There was no place to go and no road to turn off, just the side of the road. I cannot pull the car off to the side of the road and just sit there. The other car may hit us anyway. There was no safe place to go. Some people honked at this guy, and he went back into his lane.

As I passed this guy going in the opposite direction, I felt tremendous relief. I told myself we made it. The children and I are okay.

The feeling of dread was easing. I drew in a deep breath and sighed. I did not realize I was breathing shallowly until the air I was taking in felt so good.

I told the kids that everything was alright now. Of course, the boys did not know why I said that.

I looked in the mirror. What did I see? There was a large cloud of dust and car parts flying all over.

I thanked God for saving us from that accident. I prayed.

We continued home, and I felt fine. The shaking and fear went away.

We arrived home, and on the car radio, there was an announcement that Hwy 20 was close due to an accident. The road will stay closed indefinitely for the Police Investigation.

I caught the six o'clock news, and sure enough. The car accident was on TV.

The man who caused the accident was a truck driver. He was up for many hours and should not have been driving anywhere. But he had to get home. His car would have hit us and killed us if it wasn't for the people honking at him. The honking of the car's horns woke this guy up, and he did pass the children and me.

The couple driving behind us wasn't as fortunate. The couple did pass away in the accident. The truck driver had fallen asleep once again.

My life and the children's lives were spared just in the nick of time. I thanked God for intervening at the last minute and for having the people honking to wake this man up as we passed him.

Andrew

Drew was a man who had a passion for life. He was in the wrong place at the wrong time. He was twenty-one, and Drew had a passion for cars. Drew had attended Catholic Schools in a large city and had many friends.

Drew came to visit me one day with my brother shortly before his death.

My sister and I were sitting in the kitchen when my brother told me Drew was here. Drew was standing in the hallway. I went into the hall and asked Drew if he was coming in. Drew said he did not know if they were staying for a visit before they headed back to the city.

I could not believe what I was seeing. Drew had this glow all around him that amazed me to the core. I told my sister to come out and see our Drew. He had a peaceful aura. I said. "Our little Drew has grown up into this amazing man." We could not believe the transformation in him. Drew was very tall, slim and good-looking with this glow.

The visit was pleasant, with many topics of conversation.

We were sitting down at the table, and we had a conversation about Drew's life goals. The only goal he had not met was getting married and having a family. Drew said he was working on it. He had met a girl who had a baby, and he was unsure how his family would react to the relationship. Drew had not told his parents.

All of a sudden, I had a vision.

I asked Drew, "Who worked on your brakes?"

Drew replied, "The garage."

All I said was, "That is good."

I had to leave the room. I was almost in tears. I had to hold it together and return to the room. The people sitting at the table asked me. "What is wrong?"

I replied, "Nothing."

I lied. I had seen Drew die in a car accident.

We finished our visit. We hugged and kissed. Said our goodbyes.

I said, "I love you, Drew."

As Drew was on his way out the door. He promised he would be extra careful when he was driving.

As Drew was getting in the car, I said, "Drew, I love you."

My sister gave me the what's up look. She knew me.

I said, "How could I tell you that Andrew was about to die in a car accident soon."

She started to cry.

Friday night, Drew had a party to go to. He said he just had to go to the party and see all his friends from High School. Drew just had to see his friends.

Drew was having car trouble, and his car would not start all week. He kept working on the car every night after work.

Finally, Friday night, the car started. Drew drove himself to the party.

When Drew left the party early Saturday morning, he called his girlfriend and told her he would pick her up and drive her to work.

She did not answer the phone because she was getting ready for work. The Answering machine picked up the call and recorded the fatal car accident and Andrew's last words.

Instead of Drew coming home, his father answered the door, thinking Drew had forgotten his house key.

Police Officers went to where Drew lived. The Police were there to notify Drew's parents of his accident.

The Officers told his parents. Drew got caught up in a road race in which he had no part. Drew was forced off the road by cars racing. He crashed into a brick building and died instantly. The Police Officers said alcohol was not a factor in Drew's accident.

Drew had plans to spend the week with his father at the family trailer. They both had taken their holiday from work.

The girlfriend had called the Police after hearing of the accident. The Police Officers listen to Drew's recording, and they put out a request for witnesses to come forward. The people responsible for Drew's accident were never found and brought to justice.

I see Drew's Spirit frequently sitting on my couch watching TV, as he used to do before his death.

Victoria Weekend is one of the worse weekends when there are plenty of car accidents. After the long winter and spring, the long weekend in May is a promise that summer is around the corner.

After the Funeral

After my Granddaughter's Funeral, my husband and I drove my daughter and her husband home. We stayed a little while, and then we asked my daughter to go and rest, so we left.

At my daughter's house, odd things were starting to happen. Some of the people noticed and spoke of them.

The most memorable one was when my daughter woke later that night. She saw a Spirit all dressed in white standing in the doorway of her son's room. He was going to share the room with his little sister.

Seeing the Spirit frightened her, and she tried to wake up her husband so she could use the restroom. Her husband did not respond. She did not know what to make of the Spirit's visitation.

Her son was not at home at the time. I took him home with me so his mother could recover from the birth and death of her second child.

My daughter was having a difficult time dealing with her daughter's death. All her children grew up knowing they had a sister who died shortly after her birth.

My daughter had a difficult pregnancy from the start. I knew from the beginning that this child was not going to survive. My intuitive instincts were kicking in.

A couple of days before the funeral, my daughter's husband called me, and asked me to come to pick them up, and take my daughter to the hospital.

At the hospital, when I was alone with the child's father. I told him I did not think the baby would make it. I would at least try to prepare one of them for their daughter's upcoming death. He did not know what to think of my prediction. Of course, I did not tell my daughter.

The Doctors did tell us if the little girl lived. She would have been a child of special needs, and it is a blessing the child did not survive. I do not know if this is true or if they were trying to make it easier for all of us to come to terms with the little girl's death.

Angel Prevents Injury

It was like any other Friday. I finished work and picked up my grandson, he was coming to visit for the weekend. He loves to come out to the country on weekends and whenever he had time off school.

We were heading out of the city. The traffic was starting to get heavy as rush hour was approaching.

One of the favourite things the grandson loves to do is stop at Tim Horton's to get a hot chocolate and a box of donuts. We went into Tim Horton's and placed our order.

We were waiting for our turn to leave the parking lot. The traffic was heavy at this intersection. Another driver was trying to help direct me out of the driveway. He was watching the traffic to let me know when it was clear for me to make my left-hand turn. The man waved to me to proceed. I was watching and approaching cautiously. Without warning, a man came speeding up the shoulder of the road. Any person knows that you are not to use the shoulder of the road as the roadway.

The man directed me, and I did not see this car until it was almost too late. I braced for impact by putting my arm in front of my grandson to prevent him from being propelled forward.

As I was protecting my grandson, I was not concerned for myself when the car impacted the truck I was driving. As my body moved forward, I felt a force pushing me back in my seat. The invisible force was like no other sensation I had felt before.

We got out of the truck, and my grandson was crying. I asked him if he was hurt. He said, "No, I am not hurt." I checked him out, and he had no injuries.

The grandson was still crying and pointing at me. He said, "You are bleeding, Papa."

I looked down, and I saw I had red on my uniform. I said, "I am okay. It is the red jelly from the donuts." The grandson did not believe me. I put my finger in the jelly and showed him it was not blood.

To this day, I believe it was an Angel protecting me when I was keeping my grandson from injury.

We were both shaken up, a little scared, but uninjured. The grandson said. "The truck is hurt."

You see, the grandson was four at the time. I said, "That is okay. We will get the truck fixed."

S.K

Bird Man Standing Behind Nana

When my Grandchildren were young, I would bring them home to visit.

The children were playing in their bedroom, and I went in to help them put their toys away for the night.

After we finished cleaning up, the children changed into their PJs and then it would be time to read them a story.

That night my younger grandson said. "Nana, a man is standing behind you." I could feel the Spirit. I never said anything. I turned and smiled in the direction behind me.

I asked Michael, "Do you know who the man is?"

Mike said, "He did not know. The man is always here. The man likes to play with us."

The older grandson Matthew, said. "It's Bird Man." I smiled at Mike.

I took the children into the hallway. I have family pictures on the wall.

I asked Mike, "Do you see the man in these pictures?"

Mike said, "There is the man. That man is right there."

Matthew said, "Mike, I told you it is Bird Man."

The granddaughter said, "He watches me when I sleep. I get scared and go sleep with you and Papa."

I look back and say, "Hi, Dad."

I tell the children, "There is no reason to be afraid. It is Grandpa, and he won't hurt you. Grandpa likes to come and visit us."

Mike said, "He likes to play with our toys with us. He goes to our house too."

Matt said, "I have seen Bird Man at our house."

Bumps in the Night

Many things go on in this world that people shrug off and pay no attention to. They go on with what they are doing. I am no stranger to the unseen world of Spirits and Ghosts. I also have experiences with Paranormal activities. From an early age, I could see and hear the Spirit World.

I was awakened in the middle of the night many times to things that go bump in the night.

The sounds of doors opening and closing on their own were frequent. The wooden stairs leading to the basement creaked every night with the sound of someone walking up and down them. I heard Spirits or Ghosts walking through the house any time of day or night.

I could not only hear the Spirits or Ghosts walking, but I also could see them sitting on the furniture watching television. The Spirits watch me doing housework or working with clients.

When I had clients in, the Spirits or Ghosts would materialize in front of the clients to make their presence known. Whether the Spirits or Ghosts thought it was funny or the Spirits wanted me to see them. They do not frighten me. The Spirits will startle me at times.

When the Spirits did materialize, I thought they were protecting me from possible harm.

Some clients would ask to use the facilities, and I could hear them pull the shower curtains back to see if someone was behind them. I thought that was quite funny.

There is that constant sound of hearing of music playing when no radio or television is on.

Many times, clients would ask me who was in the house. I would tell them, "No one, it's just me." They would reply, "Are you sure? I could have sworn I had seen someone walk down the hall."

I would reply, "Oh, it's my father. Dad likes to come and visit me." That comment would spook some of my clients. Most of my clients knew my father had passed away. A conversation would always start about the Spirit World.

The house was not that old when my husband and I bought it. The house only had one previous owner. We lived there for thirty-one years. In all that time, we always had the constant activity of the Spirit World.

My husband and I would see the previous owners over the years. I asked them if they had a death in the house or any unusual activity. They would always answer with a definite no.

I first noticed the activity the first time we went to see the house before we bought it. As we were going through the house, someone was watching us. It was not the owners. The owners gave us the freedom to go through the house by ourselves.

We went outside, and the feeling persisted. I thought the owners were watching out of the window. Maybe they were.

We went down to the basement with the owners, and the feeling persisted. There was something else there, a Ghost, and he didn't want us there. The owners showed us city folks the ins and outs of country living.

The day we moved into the house, there was that feeling of the watchful eye persisting. My daughter noticed the presence, especially when she was in the basement. She said that there was something down there.

My husband and son didn't say too much. I guess they didn't notice anything unusual, or it did not bother them.

I would go down to the basement to do laundry. I would do it as fast as possible. I could not get back upstairs fast enough.

The tapping of metal on the basement floor would wake me. Night after night, the tapping would go on. I tried to ignore it. Finally, one night I got out of bed and told the Ghost to knock it off. "We are trying to sleep." My husband thought it was weird. He did not hear the tapping.

Things started to get worse, the constant activity. I tried to keep it under control by putting salt at the four corners of the house, and at all the doors and window openings. I blessed every room in the house. I told the Ghost he was not welcome and to leave and not return. I had a cross up in every room of the house already. I put the crosses up when we first moved in.

Things did quiet down, but not for long, then that cranky man was back tapping on the basement floor again.

There was too much activity to be just one Spirit living in the house with us.

I knew most of the spirits that were living with us were family.

Did my clients bring their family spirits with them? Did they take their ghosts or spirits with them when they went home? That is a good question. Did their Ghosts or Spirits attach themselves to me?

Coke Can

One morning a woman was going about her day of cleaning the house before leaving for work.

The woman gathered the things she needed for work, and when she was leaving, she spotted a can of coke standing up in the middle of the veranda floor.

She put her things in her car. She returned to the house. She picked up the can of coke and checked it out, and the can was still closed.

Since this was early morning, she did not have a clue. Who would leave an unopened can of coke there? Later that day, she called around to find out who had left her the coke.

Everyone she had talked to that day said it was not them. So, the mystery went on.

She remarked to a few people, "They left the coke. Where is the rum?"

They still do not know who left the can of coke. In speculation, they did come up with a plausible explanation. Was it a sign from her brother? The brother used to drink rum and coke before his passing.

Hearing Music

I was talking to a woman about the paranormal events that day. The woman was quite interested in the topic.

She was surprised that I believed in the subject. I told her I not only believed in the paranormal. I also wrote a book about it.

The woman was going to have some medical test done, and she was nervous, you can imagine.

The woman was hearing music that she had not heard in a while. These songs reminded her of her family. She thought this was interesting that nostalgia started to take over her mind. She did not mind the memories were pleasant and comforting.

She went to the hospital. She was sitting in the waiting room waiting for her test. As nervous as she was, she was listening to the music. There was a song that caught her attention, and it was very comforting for her. The song's lyrics said that she was not alone, and they were there with her, and everything was going to be alright. The song playing reminded her of her departed loved ones, her parents. The song did help take the edge off.

Everything did turn out Okay.

Finding Feathers

The one house I lived in had quite a bit of paranormal activity. At first, I was terrified to live in this house.

Right after I moved in, I went around blessing the house. The first week I lived in this house, there was a knock on the door. I answered the door to a Catholic Priest, who came to visit and welcome us to the Parish. He asked if I would like the house blessed. I was more than happy to have the house blessed by a professional.

One day after I cleaned the whole house from top to bottom, I went into my bedroom and found feathers. I could not figure out why there were feathers. I did not have anything in the house that contained feathers.

I spoke to my aunt, and she told me, "It was a sign of an Angel visiting or staying nearby in case I needed help. The Angel was protecting the children and me."

After my aunt told me this, I did some research on Angels. My aunt was right.

Angels can only appear in one place at a time. Angels are Spiritual remarkable beings of God's creations, and they will show up in time of someone's need. No one knows how many Angels are in the Universe, and there are too numerous to assign a number. Angels can make an appearance in a physical form and help you, then disappear as fast as they came.

There were numerous times I found feathers in my house, and I said, "Thank you, God, for sending your Angels to look after my children and me."

Manicotti

I was having a Book Talk at the local library, and my neighbour came to the Book Talk to support me.

Halfway through the night, the man started to tell us one of his unusual events with the paranormal. He was not a big believer in the paranormal. His wife is a believer.

They were travelling and stopped to grab a bite to eat.

He looked at the menu hanging on the wall above the cash. On the menu, the only thing he saw displayed was Manicotti. He looked away a few times, and every time he looked back at the menu, all he saw was Manicotti. So, he ordered the Manicotti for supper. He did not think very much of the incident at the time.

When he reflects on this event, he remembers, he had an aunt who passed away a few years back. In his opinion, his aunt used to make the best Manicotti. He loved his aunt and her Manicotti.

Whenever his aunt would make Manicotti, she would telephone and tell him she had Manicotti for him. He would go over for a visit and pick up the Manicotti.

He missed visiting his aunt and her Manicotti.

He ate his Manicotti for dinner and remarked that it was made and tasted very similar to his Aunt's Manicotti.

I told him his aunt was trying to get his attention and let him know that she was right there with him.

Nail in the Middle of the Bed

A woman spent the day cleaning her house and changing her bedding. When she was finished for the day, she went out.

Later that night, she returned home.

She was getting ready to go to bed, she started to pull down the covers. She noticed a nail on top of the blankets. She looked at the finishing nail in puzzlement and began searching for where it came from, and how it landed on her bed. She inspected the ceiling and the wall closest to the bed. There were no nail holes to be found.

The nail could not have come from renovations. The brother completed the renovations a couple of years before his passing.

No one had access to her home, so that was out of the question.

She thought it was bazaar how the nail appeared from nowhere.

The next day she was talking to her sister about the nail.

The only solution they came up with. Was it a sign from their father or brother?

Her father would tinker around with minor repairs, and he passed many years before this nail incident, or maybe it was a sign from her brother? Now, the brother was notorious for helping people renovate their homes. They had done some upgrades on this house before his passing. The sisters thought no more about the nail incident until I asked if they had any strange unexplainable events happen around them.

Was the nail left there by her father's spirit?

Now was the nail left there by her brother's spirit?

Passport

A woman was taking a trip to Florida to see her sister and brother-in-law.

She arrived at the Airport, checked in, and then went to Customs. Customs wanted to search her belongings. The woman could not believe that Customs targeted her for a random search. She was getting very nervous and started to cry as they went through everything. She thought it was taking them a long time to do the search. The woman finally could not take the suspense any longer. She asked the Officer if she was going to jail. Still the woman could not think of any reason why they would be searching through her belongings.

The Officer told her she could continue on her trip, and she left the search room dabbing her tears away.

Her flight went off without incident until she landed in Florida.

When the woman was getting ready to depart the plane, she took out her passport and placed it on her seat. She gathered her belongings and then went to pick up her passport. The book was not sitting on her chair.

She went through her bags, and she did not find the passport. She searched through everything several times, and then she started to cry. The other passengers sitting nearby started to help her, and they went through her stuff. They did not find the passport. Someone new to the search searched through the bags and found the passport book.

The person sitting next to her said she saw the woman with her passport book out, before she started to get ready to depart from the plane.

Why did it take several people, and the woman to search for her passport? Then the passport suddenly appeared on the seat.

That incident left many people scratching their heads and wondering why so many could not find that passport.

Seeing Angels

The first NDE was when I was a child. I was living on the Canadian Air and Arm Force Base.

I was six years old when I came down with the Influenza Flu. My father had taken me to the hospital twice, and the hospital sent me home. On the third emergency visit, the doctors admitted me to the hospital. By this time, I was very sick and not expected to live.

A Catholic Priest came in every afternoon to visit and sit with me. I remember we used to pray every day. I had almost no visitors except for the Priest and my father. My dad came to the hospital when he could.

One afternoon the Priest came to my room and gave me the Last Rites. I was only six and did not know what the Last Rites were.

That was the day I saw the Angels.

I fell asleep, and the Priest had left my room.

Later that afternoon, I awakened, and my hospital room was very bright. In the light, I saw Angels moving about my room. I was talking to them. Then I fell back to sleep. When I awakened, the Angels were gone.

I asked the nurses where are the Angels. They said that no Angels were visiting me that day.

The cleaning staff found feathers when they cleaned my room.

I found feathers in my bed.

I know many people do not see Angels or believe in them. I am one of many, who have seen Angels, and no one on earth will ever change my mind.

Angels do exist.

The Crucifix

I received a Crucifix for my Holy Communion and Confirmation. This crucifix has always hung on my bedroom wall above my bed.

One night, when I was praying, I asked God and Jesus how people could be cruel and murder each other.

Later that night, after I had fallen asleep, I had a vivid awakening. I remember looking at the crucifix, and I saw the Spirit of Jesus leave the cross. I was so shocked and could not believe my eyes. It must have been Jesus's way of telling me he was not on the cross.

When I told my aunt what had happened, boy, was she mad. She told me Jesus is not on the cross. Jesus died for our sins. Jesus's Spirit is everywhere, and his Spirit is inside every one of us. Of course, I knew that Jesus was not on the cross. I grew up with Catholic Faith.

Was Jesus reminding me after all these years that he was here and not to lose faith, and I still had work to do on his behalf?

I need to shine the light.

The Angels, Jesus, and Heaven will always be there.

You must have faith and shine your light by speaking out about your experiences and the Spiritual World.

The Hike

One day I went on a hike in a well-known Scouts Canada Camp. I knew the camp was within driving distance because I go there as a Cub Pack Leader.

On this day, I was feeling out of sorts. I needed clarity on the direction in which my life was starting to move.

A couple of years before, my then-girlfriend passed away after a long illness.

After my girlfriend's passing, my life took a dramatic shift. I started drinking and not caring about much of anything. I continued to work, and my days and drinking blended.

I went to a friend's house to visit one day. We played cards, and my friend's friend came to visit. The three of us continued to play cards together for several months. A friendship happened.

I thought about asking the woman on a date, and I did not know what to do.

Was this the appropriate time to have a relationship? Would the girl who passed away understand if I was to date someone new?

I was getting more confused and needed to put some perspective on this situation.

I drove up to this rural area and started to walk and walk. As I was walking and thinking of the girl, she happened to appear in front of me. I could not believe my eyes. She was there with me.

We had a conversation about how I was feeling. The spirit of my girlfriend told me to move on and be happy.

I did move on with some reluctance. I catch myself dwelling in the past instead of focusing on the present time and future. I have made strides in moving on.

Every year at the same time, I fall into this melancholy for a while and start acting differently. I get lost in the past.

My wife sees my previous girlfriend's spirit frequently. She rolls over and goes back to sleep. The next day my wife will ask if I had a pleasant visit with the woman's spirit. I would always tell her I did not see her spirit.

One night the woman's spirit came, and my wife spoke to her and asked. "What is the message you want me to give him?"

The woman's spirit said. "I cannot reach him. He does not know that I come to visit."

I said. "I ask him whenever you visit. How was the visit? He does say he never sees you."

Woman's spirit. "Please tell him to move on and let me go. If he doesn't, he will not be happy."

My wife relayed her message as promised.

I am more open now to acknowledge and speak to her when she visits.

S. K

The Salon

One day, I went to get my hair cut. I was feeling okay before I walked into the establishment. I was sitting there waiting for my time to be called to get my eyebrows done and my hair cut, and suddenly I did not feel so well.

The Hair Dresser called me and we went into the back room to do my eyebrows. I had my eyes closed. I opened them because I could sense that the woman and I were not alone.

I was startled at what I saw. I did not want to alarm the woman. I did not know if she knew she had ghosts in the salon.

While we were talking, the subject started to focus on my first book and the topic of Psychic Abilities.

She asked me if I sensed anything in the salon. I said yes!

She began to tell me this story.

One night her husband was in the salon by himself doing renovations, and something happened. He ran out of the salon and said he would not return.

I do not know if they hired someone to complete the renovations. The husband could have completed the work himself. If he did, I do not think he was ever in the salon by himself at night again.

The wife said her husband was frightened.

The woman said there were a couple of other Psychics in the salon before, and they said there was a presence. The Ghosts are a man and a woman. They were right. I saw them when I looked up while I was getting my eyebrows done.

The woman's ghost was a grayish-white mist, and the man's ghost was a black mist. The man was not pleasant to the woman. She was terrified of him.

The man's ghost realized I could see him. He vanished very quickly and took the woman's ghost with him.

I was shaking and wanted to get out of there fast.

We went into the next room, and I had my hair cut. I felt ill.

I got ready to leave. I put on my jacket and tried to zip it up. I was thinking to myself. I felt fine this morning. Why did I feel so ill now? Then I remembered that ghosts make you feel sick.

The woman asked me if I needed help with the zipper, I said no, and I was fine. I managed to get my jacket zipped up. I said goodbye and thanked her, and left the salon.

My husband was waiting in the vehicle. I got in, and told him there were two ghosts in the salon.

I felt guilty about leaving the woman and not trying to help get rid of the ghosts. I called the salon, and the woman was not there. Something was calling me to do something for this woman.

When I could not get a hold of this woman, I decided to try to get rid of the ghosts remotely. I tried for a week. It did not matter what time of day it was I kept trying.

I told the man ghost to let the woman ghost go. Eventually, he let the woman's spirit go. I told him to get out of the salon. That he no longer belonged there and that he was dead. Go and never return.

I have been back to this salon three or four times since, and talked to different hairdressers. I told them I tried to get rid of the ghost remotely. Each one has said that the atmosphere in the salon changed, and they cannot feel the presence any longer.

I was happy to hear that. The women who work there thanked me.

Printed in the United States
by Baker & Taylor Publisher Services